PHRASE BOOK

Compiled by
LEXUS
with
Mami Crocket
and
Tom Mitford

HARRAP
London Paris

First published in Great Britain 1990
by HARRAP BOOKS LTD
Chelsea House, 26 Market Square,
Bromley, Kent BR1 1NA

ISBN 0 245-54938-2

Printed in Great Britain by
Richard Clay (The Chaucer Press) Ltd,
Bungay, Suffolk

30

CONTENTS

The phrase sections in this book are concise and to the point. In each section you will find: a list of basic vocabulary; a selection of useful phrases; a list of common words and expressions that you will see on signs and notices. A full pronunciation guide is given for things you'll want to say or ask and typical replies to some of your questions are listed.

Of course, there are bound to be occasions when you want to know more. So this book allows for this by giving an English-Japanese dictionary with a total of some 1,600 references. This will enable you to build up your Japanese vocabulary and to make variations on the phrases in the phrase sections.

As well as this we have given a menu reader covering about 200 dishes and types of food – so that you will know what you are ordering! And, as a special feature, there is a section on colloquial Japanese.

The section on Japan and Things Japanese gives cultural information about Japan as well as some notes on the language.

For pronunciation this book uses a modified form of the standard Hepburn romanization of Japanese.

Speaking the language can make all the difference to your trip. So:

好運を祈ります！

kō un o inorimas!
good luck!

and

どうぞご無事で！

dōzo gobuji de!
have a good trip!

PRONUNCIATION

In the phrase sections of this book a pronunciation guide has been given by writing the Japanese words as though they were English. If you read out the pronunciation as English words a Japanese should be able to understand you. Some notes on the pronunciation system:

a	as in 'hard'
e	as in 'get'
i	as in 'Nagasaki'
o	as in 'hot'
u	as in 'put'

ae	pronounced 'ah-eh'
ai	pronounced as in 'Thai'
ei	pronounced as in 'freight'
ie	pronounced 'ee-eh'
ue	pronounced 'oo-eh'

g	is hard as in 'geisha'
s	as in 'mass'
y	is always as in 'you' and never as in 'why'

A bar over a vowel doubles its length. This can sometimes affect meaning. For example, 'oji·san' means 'uncle' but ojī·san' means 'grandfather'.

In spoken Japanese certain sounds are clipped. In this book we have tried to show this. For example, where older methods of romanization will give 'shita' and 'desu' we have given 'shta' and 'des' — which is how the words are actually pronounced.

Japanese pronunciation is very level. For example, when saying 'Nagasaki' all three 'a' sounds should have the same value.

It is important to remember that a final 'e' always has its full sound. For example, 'kore' (this) is pronounced 'ko-reh' and not as in English 'core'.

GENERAL PHRASES

hello
kon·nichi wa
こんにちわ

hi
dōmo dōmo
どうもどうも

good morning
ohayō gozaimas
おはようございます

good evening
komban wa
こんばんわ

good night
oyasmi nasai
おやすみなさい

pleased to meet you
hajimemashte
はじめまして

goodbye
sayōnara
さようなら

cheerio
bai bai
バイバイ

see you
ja, mata
じゃ、また

yes
hai
はい

no
īe
いいえ

yes please
hai, onegai shimas
はい、お願いします

no thank you
īe, kek·kō des
いいえ、結構です

GENERAL PHRASES

please
(*requesting*) onegai shimas
お願いします

please do
dōzo
どうぞ

thank you/thanks
arigatō
ありがとう

thanks very much
hontōni arigatō
本当にありがとう

you're welcome
dō itashimashte
どういたしまして

sorry
sumimasen
すみません

sorry? (*didn't understand*)
nan des ka?
何ですか？

how are you?
ogenki des ka?
お元気ですか？

very well, thank you
hai, okagesama de
はい、おかげさまで

and yourself?
sochira mo ogenki des ka?
そちらもお元気ですか？

excuse me (*to get attention*)
sumimasen
すみません

how much is it?
ikra des ka?
いくらですか？

can I ...?
... dekimas ka?
・・・できますか？

can I have ... ?
... o kudasai
・・・をください

I'd like to ...
...·tai des (*see grammar*)
・・・―たいです

GENERAL PHRASES

where is . . .?
. . . wa doko des ka?

・・・はどこです
か？

it's not . . .
. . . ja arimasen

・・・じゃありま
せん

is it . . .?
. . . des ka?

・・・ですか？

is there . . . ?
. . . wa arimas ka?

・・・はあります
か？

could you say that again?
mō ichido it·te kudasai

もう一度言ってく
ださい

please don't speak so fast
yuk·kuri, onegai shimas

ゆっくり、お願い
します

I don't understand
wakarimasen

わかりません

OK
ōkē

オーケー

come on, let's go!
sā, ikimashō!

さあ、行きまし
ょう！

what's that in Japanese?
Nihon·go dewa nan to
īmas ka?

日本語では何と言
いますか？

could you write that down?
kaite kudasai

書いてください

GENERAL PHRASES

I don't speak Japanese
Nihon·go ga wakarimasen

日本語がわかり
ません

that's fine!
kek·kō des

結構です

空	aki **vacant**	子供	kodomo **child**
米	Bei **USA, American**	故障	koshō **out of order**
出口	deguchi **way out**	日	Nichi **Japan, Japanese**
英	Ei **Britain, British**	日本人	Nihon·jin **Japanese**
外国人	gaikoku·jin **foreigners**	女	on·na **women**
閉	hei **closed**	押	os **push**
非常口	hijō·guchi **emergency exit**	お手洗い	otearai **toilet**
引	hik **pull**	男	otoko **men**
入口	iriguchi **way in**	大人	otona **adult**
・・・人	. . . jin **person**	使用中	shiyōchū **engaged**
開	kai **open**	立入禁止	tachi·iri kinshi **no entry**
関係者以外 の立入禁止	kankei·sha igai no tachi·iri kinshi **no admittance for unauthorized personnel**		

airport
kūkō
空港

harbour
minato
港

baggage
nimots
荷物

plane
hikōki
飛行機

book (*in advance*)
yoyak shimas
予約します

sleeper
shindaisha
寝台車

bus
bas
バス

station
eki
駅

docks
dok·k
ドック

taxi
takshī
タクシー

ferry
ferī
フェリー

terminal
tāminaru
ターミナル

gate (*at airport*)
tōjō guchi
搭乗口

train
densha
電車

a ticket to . . .
. . . made no kip·pu ichimai
・・・までの切符一枚

I'd like to reserve a seat
seki o hitots yoyak shtai des
席をひとつ予約したいです

smoking/non·smoking please
kitsu·en/kin·en seki o onegai shimas
喫煙／禁煙席をお願いします

a window seat please
madogawa no seki o onegai shimas
窓側の席をお願いします

COMING AND GOING

which platform is it for ...?
... yuki wa dono
purat·tohōm des ka?

・・・行きはどのプ
ラットホームですか？

what time is the next flight?
tsgi no bin wa nanji des ka?

次の便は何時です
か？

**is this the right train for
...?**
kore wa ... yuki no densha
des ka?

これは・・・行きの
電車ですか？

is this bus going to ...?
kono bas wa ... e ikimas
ka?

このバスは・・・
へ行きますか？

is this seat free?
kono seki wa aite imas ka?

この席は空いてい
ますか？

**do I have to change
(trains)?**
nori kaenakereba
narimasen ka?

乗り換えなければ
なりませんか？

is this the right stop for ...?
... e iku no ni, koko de
orite ī des ka?

・・・へ行くのにここ
で降りていいですか？

which terminal is it for ...?
... yuki wa dono
tāminaru des ka?

・・・行きはどの
ターミナルですか？

is this ticket ok?
kono kip·pu de ī des ka?

この切符でいい
ですか？

COMING AND GOING

I want to change my ticket
kip·pu o kaetai des

切符を換えたいです

thanks for a lovely stay
tanoshikat·ta des, arigatō

楽しかったです、
ありがとう

thanks very much for coming to meet me
ai ni kite krete, arigatō

会いに来てくれて、
ありがとう

well, here we are in . . .
sā, . . . ni tskimashta

さあ、・・・に着き
ました

申告するものがあ
りますか？

shinkoku suru mono ga arimas ka?
anything to declare?

開けてもいいです
か？

akete mo ī des ka?
would you mind opening this please?

案内	an·nai **information**	グリーン車	gurīn·sha **green car (first class)**
バス	bas **buses**	ホーム	hōm **platform**
駐車禁止	chūsha kinshi **no parking**	一時預か り所	ichiji·azukari·jo **left luggage**
出口	deguchi **exit**		
駅	eki **station**	遺失物取り 扱い所	ishits·buts tori·atskai·jo **lost property**

COMING AND GOING

時刻表	jikok·hyō **timetable**	指定席（券）	shtei·seki(·ken) **reserved seat (ticket)**
自由席	ji·yū·seki **unreserved seat**	出発	shup·pats **departure(s)**
回数券	kaisū·ken **book of tickets**	タクシー	takshī **taxis**
経由	keiyu **via**	到着	tōchak **arrival(s)**
切符	kip·pu **ticket**	運賃表	unchin·hyō **table of fares**
国際線	koksai·sen **international airlines**	・・・行き	... yuki **bound for ...**
国内線	kokunai·sen **domestic airlines**	有効	yūkō **valid**
空港	kūkō **airport**		

balcony
barukonī
バルコニー

bed
bed·do
ベッド

breakfast
chōshok
朝食

dinner
yūshok
夕食

dining room
shokdō
食堂

double room
daburu no heya
ダブル
の部屋

hotel (*Western-style*)
hoteru
ホテル

(*Japanese-style*)
ryokan
旅館

key
kagi
鍵

lunch
chūshok
昼食

night
yoru
夜

reception
uketske
受け付け

room
heya
部屋

shower
shawā
シャワー

single room
shinguru no heya
シングル
の部屋

with bath
bas tski
バス付き

youth hostel
yūs hosteru
ユースホ
ステル

do you have a room?
heya ga aite imas ka?
部屋が空いて
いますか？

just for one night
hitoban dake des
一晩だけです

do you have a room for one person?
hitori beya ga aite imas ka?
一人部屋が空い
ていますか？

15

GETTING A ROOM

do you have a room for two people?
ftari beya ga aite imas ka?

二人部屋が空いていますか？

we'd like to rent a room for a week
is·shūkan heya o karitai des

一週間、部屋を借りたいです

I'm looking for a good cheap room
yasui heya o sagashte imas

安い部屋を捜しています

I have a reservation
yoyaku shte arimas

予約してあります

how much is it?
ikra des ka?

いくらですか？

can I see the room please?
heya o miru koto ga dekimas ka?

部屋を見ることができますか？

does that include breakfast?
chōshok komi des ka?

朝食込みですか？

a room overlooking . . .
. . . no mieru heya

・・・の見える部屋

we'd like to stay another night
mō hitoban tomaritai des

もう一晩泊まりたいです

we will be arriving late
tsku no wa osok narimas

着くのは遅くなります

can I have my bill please?
seisan shte kudasai

精算してください

GETTING A ROOM

I'll pay cash
genkin de haraimas

現金で払います

can I pay by credit card?
kurejit·to kādo de mo ī
des ka?

クレジットカードでもいいですか？

will you give me a call at 6.30 in the morning?
asa no rokujihan ni okoshte kudasai

朝の六時半に起こしてください

at what time do you serve breakfast/dinner?
chōshok/yūshok wa nanji des ka?

朝食／夕食は何時ですか？

can we have breakfast in our room?
chōshok wa heya de tabete mo ī des ka?

朝食は部屋で食べてもいいですか？

thanks for putting us up
tomete krete arigatō

泊めてくれてありがとう

便所	benjo **toilet**	エレベーター	erebētā **lift**
ビジネスホテル	bijines·hoteru **business hotel**	婦人用	fujin·yō **ladies**
カプセルホテル	kapseru hoteru **capsule hotel**	非常口	hijō·guchi **emergency exit**
出口	deguchi **way out**	引	hik **pull**
		ホテル	hoteru **hotel**

17

GETTING A ROOM

化粧室	keshōshts **toilet**	紳士用	shinshi·yō **gents**
民宿	minshuk **guesthouse**	下	shta **down**
お風呂	ofuro **bath**	トイレ	toire **toilet**
押	os **push**	上	ue **up**
お手洗い	otearai **toilet**	受付	uketske **reception**
旅館	ryokan **Japanese-style hotel**		

EATING OUT

bill okanjō	お勘定	**menu** menyū	メニュー
bowl chawan	茶わん	**restaurant** restoran	レストラン
chopsticks hashi	箸	**salad** sarada	サラダ
dessert dezāto	デザート	**tea** ocha	お茶
drink nomimas	飲みます	**waiter** uētā	ウェーター
eat tabemas	食べます	**waitress** uētores	ウェートレス
food tabemono	食物	**water** mizu	水

a table for three, please
san·nin no tēburu o onegai shimas

三人のテーブルを
お願いします

we'd like to order
chūmon ga kimarimashta

注文が決まりました

what do you recommend?
osusume ryōri wa nan des ka?

お薦め料理は何
ですか？

I'd like ... please
... o kudasai

・・・をください

19

EATING OUT

can I have what he's having?
kare to onaji mono o kudasai

彼と同じものを
ください

waiter!
uētā·san!

ウェーターさん！

waitress!
uētores·san!

ウェートレスさん！

could we have the bill?
okanjō shte kudasai

お勘定してください

tea please
ocha o kudasai

お茶をください

tea with milk
miruk·tī

ミルクティー

that's for me
watashi no des

私のです

some more rice please
mot·to gohan o kudasai

もっとご飯を
ください

中華料理	chūka ryōri **Chinese restaurant**	スナックバー	snak·kubā **snack bar**
営業中	eigyō·chū **meals being served**	そば	soba **noodles**
自動ドア	jidō·doa **automatic door**	寿司処	sushi·dokoro **sushi restaurant**
お会計	okaikei **cashier**	天婦羅	tempura **restaurant specializing in deep-fried food**
ラーメン	rāmen **Chinese noodles**	和食	washok **Japanese restaurant**

20

General terms

熱い	atsui **hot**
中華料理	chūka ryōri **Chinese food**
上	jō **expensive selection**
割烹	kap·pō **expensive, quality restaurant**
並	nami **cheaper selection**
飲み屋	nomiya **local bar**
精進料理屋	shōjin ryōriya **vegetarian restaurant**
定食	teishok **set meal with rice, soup, pickles and main dish**
冷たい	tsumetai **cold**

Appetizers

おつまみ	otsumami **Japanese-style appetizers, usually crisps, Japanese crackers, dry roasted nuts, dried seaweed etc**
突き出し	tskidashi **hors d'oeuvre**

Bean Curd

油揚げ	abura·age **fried bean curd**
田楽	dengak **broiled bean curd on a stick**
豆腐	tōhu **bean curd**

MENU READER

Egg Dishes

茶碗蒸し	chawam·mushi **savoury 'custard' with egg and fish**
目玉焼き	medama·yaki **fried eggs**
卵（玉子）	tamago **egg**
卵豆腐	tamago·dōhu **steamed egg custard (savoury)**
卵とじ	tamago·toji **soft scrambled eggs with vegetables**
卵焼き	tamago·yaki **Japanese-style omelette**

Fish and Seafood

鯵（あじ）	aji **horse mackerel**
赤貝	akagai **arkshell**
甘鯛	amadai **tilefish**
穴子	anago **conger eel**
あさり	asari **short-necked clams**
鮑（あわび）	awabi **abalone, type of shellfish**
鮎（あゆ）	ayu **sweet smelt**
鰤（ぶり）	buri **yellowtail**
河豚（ふぐ）	fugu **blowfish**
ふぐちり	fugu·chiri **shredded blowfish in vegetable stew**
はまち	hamachi **young yellowtail**
蛤	hamaguri **clams**

MENU READER

鱧（はも）	hamo **sea eel**
平目	hirame **flounder**
ほたて貝	hotategai **scallop**
イカ	ika **squid**
いくら	ikura **salmon roe**
鰯（いわし）	iwashi **sardine**
蒲焼き	kabayaki **broiled and basted eel**
かじき	kajiki **swordfish**
牡蠣（かき）	kaki **oysters**
蟹（かに）	kani **crab**
かれい	karei **turbot**
鰹（かつお）	katsuo **bonito, tunny**
数の子	kazunoko **herring roe**
鱚（きす）	kiss **sea smelt**
小海老	ko·ebi **shrimps**
鯉（こい）	koi **carp**
鯨（クジラ）	kujira **whale**
海月（くらげ）	kurage **jellyfish**
車海老	kuruma·ebi **prawns**

MENU READER

鮪 （まぐろ）	maguro **tuna fish**
鱒 （ます）	mass **trout**
にぎり鮨	nigiri·zushi **raw fish on riceballs**
鰊 （にしん）	nishin **herring**
鰊の薫製	nishin no kunsei **smoked herring**
鯖 （さば）	saba **mackerel**
鮭	sake **salmon**
鮭の薫製	sake no kunsei **smoked salmon**
秋刀魚 （さんま）	sam·ma **Pacific saury**
刺身	sashimi **raw fish**
さざえ	sazae **top-shell**
しゃこ	shako **mantis crab shrimp**
蜆 （しじみ）	shijimi **corbicula, type of shellfish**
ししゃも	shishamo **smelt**
舌平目	shta·birame **sole**
寿司 （鮨）	sushi **raw fish on riceballs**
鱸 （すずき）	suzuki **bass**
鯛	tai **sea bream**
たこ	tako **octopus**

MENU READER

鱈（たら）	tara **cod**
飛び魚	tobi·uo **flying fish**
トロ	toro **pink belly of tuna**
鰻（うなぎ）	unagi **eel**
鰻重	unajū **broiled eel on rice**
雲丹（うに）	uni **sea urchin**

Meat and Meat Dishes

バター焼き	batāyaki **sliced beef or pork fried in butter**
豚肉	butanik **pork**
牛肉	gyūnik **beef**
ヒレ肉	hirenik **fillet**
串焼き	kushiyaki **grilled meat on skewers**
モツ	mots **tripe**
肉	nik **meat**
肉団子	nikudan·go **meatballs**
しゃぶしゃぶ	shabu·shabu **sliced beef with vegetables boiled at the table**
すき焼き	skiyaki **sliced beef with vegetables cooked at the table**
鉄板焼き	tep·panyaki **beef and vegetables grilled at the table**
トンカツ	tonkats **deep-fried pork cutlets**

MENU READER

焼肉
yakinik
fried pork marinated in soy sauce

Noodles

ちゃんぽん
champon
Chinese noodles in salty soup with vegetables

冷麦
hiya mugi
like sōmen, but served cold

ラーメン
rāmen
Chinese noodles

そうめん
sōmen
long, thin, white, wheatflour noodles

そば
soba
long, brownish noodles

うどん
udon
long, thick, white, wheatflour noodles

Poultry

鶏
niwatori
chicken

雀（すずめ）
suzume
sparrow

鳥料理
tori·ryōri
poultry dishes

鶉（うずら）
uzura
quail

焼き鳥
yakitori
barbecued chicken

Rice and Rice Dishes

炒飯
chāhan
fried rice

チキンライス
chikin rais
rice with chicken

ちらし寿司
chirashi·zushi
mixed sushi on rice, with chopped vegetables and strips of fried egg etc

・・・丼
... domburi
bowl of rice with ... on top

MENU READER

御飯
gohan
rice

ハヤシライス
hayashi rais
sliced or minced beef with rice

釜飯
kamameshi
rice steamed in fish stock with pieces of meat, fish and vegetable

カレーライス
karērais
curry rice

カツカレー
katskarē
pork cutlets with curry

カツ丼
katsudon
deep-fried pork on rice

海苔巻き
nori·maki
sliced roll of rice, vegetables and fish powder, wrapped in seaweed

お茶漬け
ochazuke
rice in tea or fish broth

オムライス
omuraiss
omelette with rice

おにぎり
onigiri
riceballs

親子丼
oyako·domburi
rice topped with chicken and onion cooked in egg

卵丼
tamago·domburi
rice topped with onion cooked in egg

鰻丼
unadon
grilled eel on rice

Seasoning and Herbs

油
abura
oil

味の素
ajinomoto (R)
flavour enhancer

がり
gari
pickled slices of ginger

味噌（みそ）
miso
fermented soybean paste

MENU READER

山椒	sanshō **Japanese pepper**
生姜	shōga **ginger**
醤油（正油）	shōyu **soy sauce**
酢	su **vinegar**
沢庵（たくあん）	takuan **yellow radish pickles**
梅干し	umeboshi **pickled plum**
わさび	wasabi **Japanese horseradish**

Seaweed

ひじき	hijiki **kind of seaweed**
昆布（こんぶ）	kombu **kind of seaweed (thick)**
海苔	nori **kind of seaweed (paper-like)**
わかめ	wakame **kind of seaweed**

Snacks, Desserts

あべかわ餅	abekawa mochi **rice cakes covered in bean powder**
かき餅	kaki mochi **small crackers with soy sauce flavouring**
カステラ	kastera **sponge cake**
饅頭（まんじゅう）	manjū **rice-flour buns with bean paste filling**
蜜豆（みつまめ）	mitsumame **gelatin cubes and sweet beans with pieces of fruit**

MENU READER

餅（もち）	mochi **rice cakes**
おはぎ	ohagi **glutinous rice and bean paste**
おせんべい	osembei **rice crackers**
お汁粉	oshiruko **sweet bean soup with rice cake**
さくら餅	sakura mochi **bean paste rice cake wrapped in cherry leaf**
和菓子	wagashi **Japanese-style sweets**
洋菓子	yōgashi **gâteau**
羊羹	yōkan **soft, sweet bean paste**
ぜんざい	zenzai **thick bean paste with whole beans and rice cakes**

Soups

ホーレン草のポタージュ	hōrensō no potāj **spinach soup**
みそ汁	misoshiru **soup with 'miso' (fermented soya bean paste)**
汁物	shirumono **soups**
吸い物	suimono **clear soup with vegetables or fish**
清汁（すましじる）	sumashijiru **clear soup with vegetables or fish**
野菜のクリームスープ	yasai no kurīm sūp **cream of vegetable soup**

MENU READER

Vegetables and Fruit

小豆（あずき）	adzuki **red beans**
大豆	daizu **soybeans**
枝豆	eda·mame **boiled green soybeans**
エンドウ豆	endō·mame **peas**
えのき茸	enokidake **yellow button mushroom**
蕗	fuki **wild butterbur**
銀杏	gin·nan **ginko nuts**
牛蒡	gobō **burdock root**
白菜	hak·sai **Chinese cabbage**
ジャガ芋	jagaimo **potato**
かぼちゃ	kabocha **marrow**
柿	kaki **persimmon**
かんぴょう	kampyō **dried gourd shavings**
菊の花	kiku·no·hana **chrysanthemum flowers**
きんぴら	kimpira **fried burdock root**
茸（きのこ）	kinoko **mushrooms (general term)**
こんにゃく	kon·nyak **arum root jelly**
果物	kudamono **fruit**
胡瓜（きゅうり）	kyūri **cucumber**

MENU READER

豆	mame **beans**
松茸	matstake **Japanese mushrooms**
芽キャベツ	mekyabets **brussels sprouts**
蜜柑（みかん）	mikan **tangerine**
もやし	moyashi **bean sprouts**
梨	nashi **pear**
茄子（なす）	nass **aubergine**
納豆	nat·tō **fermented soybeans**
葱（ねぎ）	negi **leek**
人参（にんじん）	ninjin **carrots**
ニラ	nira **scallion leek**
おひたし	ohitashi **boiled spinach with seasoning**
ピーマン	pīman **green pepper**
らっきょう	rak·kyō **scallion, served pickled**
蓮根	renkon **lotus root**
林檎（リンゴ）	rin·go **apple**
里芋	sato·imo **taro**
薩摩芋（さつま芋）	satsuma·imo **sweet potato**
さやえんどう	saya·endō **garden peas**

MENU READER

しめじ	shimeji **brown button mushrooms**
しらたき	shirataki **arum paste noodles**
ししとう	shishtō **green pepper (small)**
椎茸	shītake **dried or Chinese mushrooms**
春菊	shun·gik **chrysanthemum greens**
西瓜（すいか）	suika **watermelon**
竹の子（筍）	takenoko **bamboo shoots**
玉葱	tamanegi **onion**
山芋	yama·imo **yam**
野菜	yasai **vegetables**

HAVING A DRINK

bar bā	バー	**lemonade** saidā	サイダー
beer bīru	ビール	**orange juice** orenj jūs	オレンジ ジュース
coke (R) kōku	コーク		
dry karakchi	辛口	**rice wine** sake	酒
gin and tonic jin tonik·k	ジントニ ック	**straight** (no ice) storēto	ストレート
		sweet amakchi	甘口
ice kōri	氷	**vodka** uok·ka	ウォッカ
lager ragā bīru	ラガー ビール	**whisky** uiskī	ウィスキー
		wine wain	ワイン

let's go for a drink
nomi ni ikimashō

飲みに行きましょう

a beer please
bīru o kudasai

ビールをください

small/medium/large
shō/chū/dai

小／中／大

two beers please
bīru nihai kudasai

ビール二杯ください

a Japanese beer
Nihon no bīru

日本のビール

HAVING A DRINK

an imported beer
yunyū bīru

輸入ビール

a glass of red/white wine
aka/shiro wain o ip·pai

赤／白ワインを一杯

with lots of ice
kōri o taksan irete

氷をたくさん入れて

no ice thanks
kōri wa irenaide kudasai

氷は入れないで
ください

can I have another one?
okawari o kudasai

おかわりをください

the same again please
onaji mono o kudasai

同じものをください

what'll you have?
nani o nomimas ka?

何を飲みますか？

I'll get this round
kore wa watashi mochi des

これは私もちです

not for me thanks
mō irimasen

もういりません

he's absolutely smashed
kare wa yoi·tsburete imas

彼は酔い潰れてい
ます

バー	bā **bar**	ブランディー	brandē **brandy**
ビール	bīru **beer**	喫茶店	kis·saten **café**

HAVING A DRINK

紅茶	kōcha **black tea**	焼酎	shōchū **colourless, odourless, very strong and cheap liquor**
お飲み物	o·nomimono **beverages**		
オンザロック	onza·rok·k **scotch on the rocks**	ウィスキー	uiskī **whisky**
酒	sake **sake, Japanese rice wine**		

COLLOQUIAL EXPRESSIONS

barmy
baka baka shī

ばかばかしい

bastard
bakayarō

馬鹿野郎

bird
kawaiko chan

カワイ子ちゃん

bloke
yats

奴

nutter
kawarimono

変り者

pissed
bero bero

ベロベロ

thickie
noroma

のろま

twit
manuke

間抜け

great!
sugoi!

すごい！

that's awful!
hidoi ne!

ひどいね！

shut up!
damare!

黙れ！

ouch!
itai!

痛い！

yum·yum!
umai umai!

うまいうまい！

I'm absolutely knackered
kta kta des

クタクタです

I'm fed up
unzari des

ウンザリです

I'm fed up with ...
... ni wa unzari shimas

・・・にはウンザリします

36

COLLOQUIAL EXPRESSIONS

don't make me laugh!
owarai des
お笑いです

you've got to be joking!
jōdan deshō
冗談でしょう

it's rubbish (*goods etc*)
boro des
ボロです

it's a rip-off
hōgai·na nedan des
法外な値段です

get lost!
usero!
失せろ！

it's a damn nuisance
hidok yak·kai des
ひどく厄介です

it's absolutely fantastic
tonikak sugoi des
とにかくすごいです

馬鹿め！	bakame! **idiot!**	クソ！	kso! **shit!**
馬鹿野郎！	bakayarō! **damn fool!**	素晴らしい	subarashī! **fantastic!**
畜生！	chikshō! **hell!**	すみません	sumimasen **thanks; sorry; can I?**
どうも	dōmo **thanks; hi**	洋モク	yōmoku **foreign cigarettes**
外人	gaijin **foreigner, wog**		

GETTING AROUND

bike
jitensha
自転車

bus
bas
バス

car
kruma
車

change (*trains*)
nori·kaemas
乗り換えます

garage (*for fuel*)
gasorin stando
ガソリンスタンド

hitch-hike
hit·ch haik shimas
ヒッチハイクします

map
chiz
地図

moped
tansha
軽二輪

motorbike
baik
バイク

petrol
gasorin
ガソリン

return (ticket)
ōfuk
往復

single
katamichi
片道

station
eki
駅

taxi
takshī
タクシー

ticket
kip·pu
切符

train
densha
電車

underground
chikatets
地下鉄

I'd like to rent a car
kruma o karitai des
車を借りたいです

how much is it per day?
ichi nichi ni tski ikra des ka?
一日に付きいくらですか？

when do I have to bring the car back?
its modoshtara ī des ka?
いつ戻したらいいですか？

GETTING AROUND

I'm heading for . . .
. . . e mukat·te imas

・・・へ向かって
います

how do I get to . . .?
. . . e wa dō ikeba ī des
ka?

・・・へはどう行
けばいいですか？

REPLIES

まっすぐ

mas·sugu
straight on

左／右へ曲って

hidari/migi e magat·te
turn left/right

あそこの建物です

asoko no tatemono des
it's that building there

あっちの方です

at·chi no hō des
it's back that way

左側の一／二／
三番目

**hidarigawa no ichi/ni/san
bam·me**
first/second/third on the left

we're just travelling around
chot·to ryokō·chū des

ちょっと旅行中
です

I'm a stranger here
koko o yok shirimasen

ここをよく知り
ません

is that on the way?
sore wa tochū ni arimas
ka?

それは途中にあ
りますか？

GETTING AROUND

can I get off here?
koko de orite mo ī des ka?

ここで降りても
いいですか？

thanks very much for the lift
nosete krete arigatō

乗せてくれてあ
りがとう

two returns to . . . please
. . . made ōfuk de nimai kudasai

・・・まで往復で
二枚ください

what time is the last train back?
kaeri no saishū bin wa its des ka?

帰りの最終便はい
つですか？

we want to leave tomorrow and come back the day after
ashta dete, yokujits ni modoritai des

明日出て、翌日に
戻りたいです

we're coming back the same day
higaeri no yotei des

日帰りの予定です

is this the right platform for . . .?
koko wa . . . yuki no purat·tohōm des ka?

ここは・・・行き
のプラットホーム
ですか？

is this train going to . . .?
kono densha wa . . . yuki des ka?

この電車は・・・
行きですか？

where are we?
koko wa doko des ka?

ここはどこです
か？

GETTING AROUND

which stop is it for . . .?
. . . e wa doko de orimas ka?

・・・へはどこ
で降りますか？

how far is it to the nearest petrol station?
ichiban chikai gasorin·stando made, dono krai no kyori des ka?

一番近いガソリン
スタンドまで、
どの位の
距離ですか？

I need a new tyre
atarashī taiya ga irimas

新しいタイヤが
いります

it's overheating
ōbāhīto shte imas

オーバーヒート
しています

there's something wrong with the brakes
burēki no chōshi ga hen des

ブレーキの調子
が変です

駐車禁止	chūsha kinshi **no parking**	ひかり	hikari **faster bullet train**
出口	deguchi **exit**	入口	iriguchi **entrance**
普通	futsū **ordinary train**	徐行	jokō **slow**
東	higashi **east**	準急	jun·kyū **semi-express**
非常出口	hijō·deguchi **emergency exit**	川	kawa **river**

GETTING AROUND

禁煙 kin·en **no smoking**

北 kita **north**

こだま kodama **slower bullet train**

工事中 kōji·chū **road works**

高速道路 kōsok dōro **expressway**

急行 kyūkō **express**

満員 man·in **full**

南 minami **south**

湖 mizūmi **lake**

西 nishi **west**

お風呂 ofuro **public bath**

温泉 onsen **hot spring bath**

料金箱 ryōkim·bako **fare box**

精算所 seisan·jo **excess fare office**

市 shi **town, city**

島 shima **island**

新幹線 shinkansen **bullet train**

食堂車 shokudō·sha **dining car**

タクシー takshī **taxis**

特急 tok·kyū **special express**

通行止め tsūkō·dome **no through traffic**

海 umi **sea**

山 yama **mountain**

SHOPPING

carrier bag
fkuro
袋

cashdesk
reji
レジ

cheap
yasui
安い

cheque
kogit·te
小切手

department
uriba
売場

expensive
takai
高い

market
ichiba
市場

pay
haraimas
払います

receipt
reshīto
レシート

shop
mise
店

shop assistant
ten·in
店員

supermarket
sūpā
スーパー

I'd like ...
... ga hoshī des
・・・が欲しいです

have you got ...?
... ga arimas ka?
・・・がありますか？

how much is this?
kore wa ikra des ka?
これはいくらですか？

the one in the window
shō·windō ni aru mono
ショーウィンドーにあるもの

do you take credit cards ?
krejit·to kādo de ī des ka?
クレジットカードでいいですか？

SHOPPING

I'd like to try it on
tskete mite ī des ka?

着けてみていい
ですか？

I'll come back
modot·te kimas

戻って来ます

it's too big/small
ōki/chīsa·sugimas

大き／小さ過ぎます

I'll take it
sore ni shimas

それにします

can you gift-wrap it?
prezento yōni hōsō
shte kudasai

プレゼント用に
包装してください

文房具	bumbōgu **stationery**	レジ	reji **cashier**
電気製品	denki seihin **electrical goods**	紳士服 （売場）	shinshi·fuk (uriba) **menswear (dept)**
婦人服 （売場）	fujin·fuk (uriba) **ladies wear (dept)**	食品	shokuhin **food**
カメラ屋	kamera·ya **camera shop**	下着（売場）	shtagi (uriba) **underwear (dept)**
お勘定	okanjō **pay here**		
おもちゃ （売場）	omocha (uriba) **toys (dept)**	スポーツ 用品	spōts yōhin **sports goods**
大売出し	ō·uridash **bargains, sale**	一屋	·ya **... shop**

44

JAPAN AND THINGS JAPANESE

FESTIVALS

There are eight traditional festivals held all over Japan. These are to a large extent family and child-centred occasions.

The first and the most important is New Year. At midnight on New Year's Eve, the deep temple bells boom out 108 times, to expel the 108 desires of Buddhism. Three days official holiday follow and several more days of unofficial celebration.

February 3 is the festival that marks the beginning of spring, *Setsubun*, Bean Throwing Festival. At temples or outside their homes, children throw beans and chant *fuku wa uchi, oni wa soto* 'in with wealth, out with the devils.'

Hina Matsuri, the girls' festival, comes next, on March 3. On that day, dolls are displayed in the home for an imperial wedding with attendants, officials and musicians escorting the prince and princess.

The Buddha's birthday is celebrated on April 8.

In May, on the 5th, the boys have their festival. Special foods are prepared for them, and *koinobori*, kites shaped like carp, fly from poles above the house.

Tanabata, on July 7, is the day Vega and Altair meet in the Milky Way. They were once a Chinese cowherd and a weaving girl, unhappy lovers who became stars allowed to meet once a year.

JAPAN AND THINGS JAPANESE

Obon, in mid-July, is when the dead are honoured. They are believed to return for three days to visit their descendants in their homes.

Shichigosan, meaning 7 5 3, falls on November 15. It is a day for all children who are 3, 5 and 7 years old.

Very famous are the *Hanami* days, when families go out to enjoy the spring blossom and to have picnics. This happens for plum in February, for peach in March and cherry in March or April, the days varying from place to place depending on when the flowers are at their best.

Different areas in Japan have their own annual festivals when a shrine is carried from the temple through the streets. This carried shrine is called a *mikoshi*.

TRANSPORT

Japan has a marvellous network of railways, symbolized by the bullet trains.

It is, however, cheaper to go on slower trains, which, with windows wide open and frequent stops, give a richer impression of the countryside.

The railpass is an excellent buy, and allows free travel on many ferries. A voucher must be bought before travelling to Japan, and it is then exchanged for a railcard and date-stamped when presented at a main station.

It is also convenient to hire a car. Roads are good, but sometimes busy and fairly narrow. However, less freight is transported by road than in EEC countries.

JAPAN AND THINGS JAPANESE

There are many long-distance car ferries between all the main islands of Japan, from Kagoshima in southern Kyushu to Osaka, from Osaka through the Inland Sea to Shimonoseki, from Nishi Maizuru just north of Kyoto to Hokkaido etc. Passengers install themselves for the journey on the communal matting. Local ferries serve all the smaller islands, places seldom visited by foreigners at all, very traditional but also modern and prosperous.

It is often expensive to buy an international air ticket in Japan, and best, if possible, to purchase air tickets for onward flights before you arrive.

ACCOMMODATION

TIC, the Tourist Information Centres, are extremely helpful and will gladly advise on all kinds of accommodation. There is a TIC office at Narita Airport and another near the main railway station in Tokyo.

Traditional Japanese hotels, *ryokan*, have great character, and may be very old. Meals are served in one's room, and in the evening, the bedding is brought out from a cupboard in the wall and spread out on the matting.

There are also 'business hotels.' They are relatively inexpensive, but may be more impersonal than *ryokan*.

In the big cities, there are 'capsule hotels'. Here one stays in a large locker, with a tiny television set. These are ideal for people who need somewhere cheap to sleep.

JAPAN AND THINGS JAPANESE

It is possible all over Japan to stay in guesthouses called *minshku*. Here you can have dinner, bed and breakfast in a Japanese home.

Japan has a network of youth hostels, *yūs hosteru*, ranging from Tokyo and Osaka to remote islands. A youth hostel guide lists them all, with maps and directions.

JAPANESE WRITING

The Japanese script is exceedingly complex: four systems are used in combination.

First, there are the Chinese characters, the *kanji*, which were introduced into Japan in the third century A.D., the earliest Japanese writing.

Because the Japanese language is completely different from Chinese, the Chinese characters were not satisfactory on their own. Chinese nouns and verbs do not decline and conjugate, but Japanese verbs have many forms.

So, about five centuries later, the Japanese developed a new script, the *kana*, to supplement the *kanji*.

Thus 'I didn't go'

行きませんでした

is written with a kanji for 'go'

行

and 'kana' for 'didn't'

きませんでした

The kanji represent ideas, but the kana represent sounds (as our letters do).

JAPAN AND THINGS JAPANESE

There are two kinds of kana, the softer forms originally
written by court ladies, and the harsher forms written
by court officials, the *hiragana* and *katakana*
respectively. Today, the katakana syllables are used
for words imported from foreign languages, for
example:

オンザロック

onza·rok·k
scotch on the rocks

The fourth system is the Roman alphabet (which is
used especially for brand names).

It would certainly be possible to write Japanese in only
one script, but because the range of vowels and
consonants is not big, the different scripts are helpful
because they show immediately what is an old word
from China, what is a recent American term and what
is part of the Japanese syntax.

GETTING AROUND

At first, Tokyo is overwhelming, and it is not easy to
get around.

The Tourist Information Centre will give every
assistance, and supply maps and advice on
accommodation.

It is very useful to be able to ask basic directions in
Japanese. The pronunciation is straightforward, and a
few words help immensely. Hotels will all supply
cards with their name and address and telephone
number; it would be very easy to lose one's hotel if one
didn't have these details in writing.

JAPAN AND THINGS JAPANESE

Spoken English is not widely understood. It is the young people who are most likely to understand, and they can write down directions in Japanese for you to show the next time you need help.

In every city and town, there are local police offices. The police are courteous and helpful. They will feel responsible for you, but may make arrangements without fully understanding your needs.

In remoter places, a stranger may be ignored. It may be that people do not know how to begin to communicate with someone they assume cannot speak their language.

Shopping is easy, as many shops are self-service. Restaurant menus are greatly simplified by the plastic meals displayed in the window.

It is important to know about strict rules for wearing the right slippers in *minshku* and *ryokan*. Only special light slippers can be worn on the tatami matting. Whenever you leave the matting, you must change out of these slippers. There are always new slippers waiting for you.

It is also important not to wash in the bath. You should wash and rinse outside the bath, and then relax in the hot water. The reason for this is that fuel for heating the water used to be scarce, and so the same water was used by many people.

There are often low beams in old houses, and it is easy for a tall person to bang his head.

JAPAN AND THINGS JAPANESE

VISITING A HOME

If you visit a home, a small present will be much
appreciated. Japanese presents are exquisitely
wrapped, and usually they are not opened till later.

Many people on meeting do not shake hands. Instead,
one bows, not too deeply, and smiles. If you are
travelling on business, it is essential to carry
namecards, *meishi*, to exchange on introduction. A
card is offered with both hands, and with a slight bow,
and when it is received it should be courteously
studied.

Before a meal in a home, everyone says *itadakimas* (I
receive). This is a humble verb form, acknowledging
all the labour that has gone into growing the rice and
catching the fish. At the end of the meal, you say
gochisō·sama deshta! (it was a feast), and can add
oishikat·ta des (it was delicious).

Japanese never blow their noses loudly, so if you have
a cold, be discreet.

In general the Japanese will be too gracious to take
offence at any breach of etiquette. So if, for example,
you remove your shoes and find you have a hole in
your sock — it doesn't matter. What is important is a
general attitude of friendliness and respect.

bank ginkō	銀行
bill okanjō	お勘定
bureau de change ryōgaesho	両替所
cash dispenser genkin jidō madoguchi	現金自動窓口
change (*small*) kozeni	小銭
cheque kogit·te	小切手

credit card krejit·to kādo	クレジットカード
exchange rate ryōgae rēto	両替レート
expensive takai	高い
pounds (sterling) pondo	ポンド
price nedan	値段
receipt reshīto	レシート
yen en	円

how much is it?
kore wa ikra des ka?

これはいくらですか？

I'd like to change this into . . .
kore o . . . to kōkan·shte kudasai

これを・・・と交換してください

can you give me something smaller?
mō skoshi komakai no ni shte kudasai

もう少し細かいのにしてください

can I use this credit card?
kono krejit·to kādo de ī des ka?

このクレジットカードでいいですか？

MONEY

can we have the bill please?
okanjō o onegai shimas

お勘定をお願い
します

please keep the change
komakai no wa irimasen

細かいのはいり
ません

does that include service?
kore wa sābisryō·komi
des ka?

これはサービス
料込みですか？

**I think the figures are
wrong**
kono sūji wa machigat·te
imasen ka?

この数字は間違
っていませんか？

I'm completely skint
okane ga soko o tskimashta

お金が底をつき
ました

円	en **yen**	無料	muryō **no charge**
外国為替 公認銀行	gaikoku·kawase· kōnin·ginkō **authorized foreign exchange bank**	両替所	ryōgaejo **bureau de change**
		料金	ryōkin **fee**
銀行	ginkō **bank**	消費税	shōhizei **VAT**
いらっしゃ いませ！	iras·shaimase! **at your service (literally: come in)**	有料	yūryō **fee charged**

ENTERTAINMENT

band (*pop*)
bando — バンド

cinema
eigakan — 映画館

concert
konsāto — コンサート

disco
disko — ディスコ

film
eiga — 映画

go out
dekakemas — 出掛けます

music
on·gak — 音楽

pinball
pachinko — パチンコ

play (*theatre*)
engeki — 演劇

seat
zaseki — 座席

show
shō — ショー

singer
kashu — 歌手

theatre
gekijō — 劇場

ticket
kip·pu — 切符

are you doing anything tonight?
komban nanika yotei ga arimas ka?

今晩、何か予定が
ありますか？

do you want to come out with me tonight?
komban is·shoni dekakemasen ka?

今晩、一緒に出掛
けませんか？

what's on?
nani o yat·te imas ka?

何をやっていま
すか？

ENTERTAINMENT

have you got a programme of what's on in town?
ima machi de nani o yat·te iru ka gyōji· an·nai ga arimas ka?

今、町で何をやっているか、行事案内がありますか？

which is the best disco round here?
kokora de ichiban ī disko wa doko des ka?

ここらで一番いいディスコはどこですか？

let's go to the cinema/theatre
eiga/gekijō e ikimashō

映画／劇場へ行きましょう

I've seen it
mae ni mimashta

前に見ました

I'll meet you at 9 o'clock at the station
eki de kuji ni aimashō

駅で九時に会いましょう

can I have two tickets for tonight?
kon·ya no kip·pu o nimai kudasai

今夜の切符を二枚ください

I'd like to book three seats for tomorrow
ashta no zaseki o mit·ts yoyak shtai des

明日の座席をみっつ予約したいです

do you want to dance?
odorimasen ka?

踊りませんか？

do you want to dance again?
mō ichido odorimasen ka?

もう一度踊りませんか？

ENTERTAINMENT

thanks but I'm with my boyfriend
zan·nen des ga, bōifrendo to is·sho na no de

残念ですが、ボーイフレンドと一緒なので

let's go out for some fresh air
soto no kūki ni atarimashō

外の空気にあたりましょう

will you let me back in again later?
mata ato de naka e irete moraemas ka?

また後で中へ入れて貰えますか？

I'm meeting someone inside
naka ni iru hito ni aimas

中にいる人に会います

ディスコ	disko **disco**	パチンコ	pachinko **pinball**
ゲームセンター	gēm·sentā **amusement arcade**	ポルノ	poruno **pornography**
上映中	jōeichū **now showing**	成人映画	seijin·eiga **adult film**
カラオケ	kara·oke **karaoke bar**		

BUSINESS

business shigoto	仕事	**meeting** kaigō	会合
business card meishi	名刺	**price** nedan	値段
company kaisha	会社	**quote** (*noun*) mitsumori	見積もり
contract keiyaku	契約	**target** mok·hyō	目標
fax (*noun*) fak·ks	ファックス	**telex** terek·ks	テレックス
instalment bunkats barai	分割払い	**workflow** **schedule** tejun no skejūru	手順のス ケジュール
invoice seikyūsho	請求書		
managing **director** shachō	社長		

I have a meeting with Mr ... ...san to aimas	・・・さんと会 います
may I introduce Mr ...? ...san o shōkai shimas	・・・さんを紹介 します
he is our technical director/sales director uchi no gijuts buchō/hanbai buchō des	うちの技術部長／ 販売部長です

BUSINESS

could you give me your fax number?
fak·ks no ban·gō o oshiete kudasai

ファックスの
番号を教えて
ください

I'd like to have time to think it over
kangaeru jikan o kudasai

考える時間を
ください

we're very excited about it
watashitachi mo hijōni kitai shte imas

私達も非常に期待
しています

I'm afraid this is still a problem
kore wa mada muzkashī tokoro des

これはまだ難しい
ところです

ok, that's a deal
jā, kore de te o uchimashō

じゃあ、これで手
を打ちましょう

let's drink to a succesful partnership
o·tsuki·ai no seikō o inot·te nomimashō

お付き合いの成功
を祈って飲みま
しょう

it's a pleasure doing business with you
o·torihiki ga dekite ureshī des

お取引が出来て
嬉しいです

accident jiko	事故	**fire brigade** shōbōsha	消防車
ambulance kyūkyūsha	救急車	**ill** byōki no	病気の
broken orete	折れて	**injured** kega o shte	怪我をして
doctor o·isha	お医者	**late** osoi	遅い
emergency kinkyū	緊急	**out of order** kowarete	壊れて
fire kaji	火事	**police** keisats	警察

can you help me? I'm lost
michi ni mayoimashta,
tasukete kudasai

道に迷いました、
助けてください

I've lost my passport
paspōto o nakshimashta

パスポートをな
くしました

I'm looking for . . .
. . . o sagashte imas

・・・を捜して
います

I can't get it open
akimasen

開きません

it's jammed
nanika tskaete imas

何か、つかえて
います

PROBLEMS

I've locked myself out of my room
heya no kagi o naka ni okip·panashide shimete shimaimashta

部屋の鍵を中に置きっぱなしで、閉めてしまいました

my luggage hasn't arrived
nimots ga mada tskimasen

荷物がまだ着きません

I don't have enough money
okane ga tarimasen

お金が足りません

I've broken down
kruma ga enko shimashta

車がエンコしました

this is an emergency
kinkyū jitai des

緊急事態です

help!
taskete!

助けて！

it doesn't work
kowarete imas

壊れています

the lights aren't working in my room
heya no denki ga tskimasen

部屋の電気が点きません

the lift is stuck
erebētā ga ugokimasen

エレベーターが動きません

I can't understand a single word
hitokoto mo wakarimasen

一言もわかりません

can you get an interpreter?
tsūyak o sagashte kudasai

通訳を捜してください

PROBLEMS

the toilet won't flush
toire no mizu ga
nagaremasen

トイレの水が流
れません

there's no toilet paper left
toire ni mō kami ga
arimasen

トイレにもう紙
がありません

**I'm afraid I've accidentally
broken the . . .**
sumimasen . . . o kowashte
shimaimashta

すみません、・・・
を壊してしま
ました

**my handbag has been
stolen**
watashi wa handobag·g o
nusumaremashta

わたしはハンドバ
ッグを盗まれまい
した

注意	chūi **caution**	高圧	kō·ats **high voltage**
非常口	hijō·guchi **emergency exit**	故障	koshō **out of order**
避難口	hinan·guchi **emergency exit**	・・・お断り	・・・okotowari **. . . forbidden**
警察	keisats **police**	立入禁止	tachi·iri kinshi **keep out**
危険	kiken **danger**		

English	Rōmaji	Japanese
acupuncture	hari	針
bandage	hōtai	包帯
blood	chi	血
broken	orete	折れて
burn	yakedo	火傷
chemist's	ksuri·ya	薬屋
contraception	hinin·yak	避妊薬
dentist	ha·isha	歯医者
disabled	shintai shōgaisha	身体障害者
disease	byōki	病気
doctor	o·isha	お医者
health	kenkō	健康
hospital	byōin	病院
ill	byōki (no)	病気（の）
nurse	kangofu	看護婦

I don't feel well
kibun ga warui des

気分が悪いです

it's getting worse
mae yori mo hidok nat·te imas

前よりもひどく
なっています

I feel better
mae yori mo yok narimashta

前よりもよく
なりました

I feel sick
haki·ke ga shimas

吐き気がします

I've got a pain here
koko ga itai des

ここが痛いです

HEALTH

it hurts
itamimas

痛みます

he's got a high temperature
kare wa nets ga arimas

彼は熱があります

could you call a doctor?
o·isha o yonde kudasai

お医者を呼んで
ください

is it serious?
jūshō des ka?

重症ですか？

will he need an operation?
kare ni wa shujuts no
hitsyō ga arimas ka?

彼には手術の必
要がありますか？

I'm diabetic
watashi wa tōnyōbyō
des

私は糖尿病です

have you got anything for …?
… ni kik ksuri ga arimas
ka?

・・・に効く薬
がありますか？

病院	byōin **hospital**	産婦人科	sanfujinka **obstetrics and gynaecology**
眼科	ganka **eye department**	診療時間	shinryō·jikan **consultation hours**
外科	geka **surgery (operations)**	歯科	shka **dentistry**
医院	īn **(small) hospital**	小児科	shōnika **paediatrics**
耳鼻咽喉科	jibi·inkōka **ear, nose and throat department**		

63

can we play table-tennis?
pin·pon o shimashō ka?

ピンポンをしま
しょうか？

I'm going jogging
jog·ging·g ni ikimas

ジョッギングに
いきます

we want to go on a bicycle trip
saikring·g ni ikitai des

サイクリングに
行きたいです

let's go swimming
oyogi ni ikimashō

泳ぎに行き
ましょう

I want learn some judo
jūdō o naraitai des

柔道を習いた
いです

I'd like to see some sumo wrestling
smō o mini ikitai des

相撲を見に行き
たいです

I'd like to see a martial arts demonstration
bujuts no jitsu·en o mitai des

武術の実演を見
たいです

this is the first time I've ever tried it
yat·te mitano wa kore ga hajimete des

やってみたのはこ
れが初めてです

THE POST OFFICE

letter
tegami
手紙

parcel
kozutsmi
小包み

post office
yūbin·kyok
郵便局

registered
kakitome yūbin
書留郵便

send
okurimas
送ります

stamp
kit·te
切手

telegram
dempō
電報

how much is a letter to Ireland?
Airurando made fūsho no kit·tedai wa ikra des ka?

アイルランドまで
封書の切手代は
いくらで
すか？

I'd like four 80 yen stamps
hachijū en no kit·te o yom·mai kudasai

八十円の切手を
四枚ください

I'd like six stamps for postcards to England
Igiris ate no hagaki ni haru kit·te o rokmai kudasai

イギリス宛ての
葉書に貼る切手を
六枚ください

is there any mail for me?
watashi ate ni tegami ga kite imas ka?

私宛てに手紙が来
ていますか？

THE POST OFFICE

I'm expecting a parcel from ...
... kara no kozutsmi ga kru hazu des

・・・からの小包み が来るはずです

can I send this express?
kore o soktats de okremas ka?

これを速達で送れますか？

can I send this registered?
kore o kakitomebin de okremas ka?

これを書留便で送れますか？

電報	dempō **telegram**	速達	soktats **express mail**
切手	kit·te **stamp**	郵便局	yūbin·kyok **post office**
航空便	kōkūbin **airmail**	〒 ☺	symbols for Japanese post office
小包み	kozutsumi **parcel, package**		

TELEPHONING

directory enquiries
denwa ban·gō an·nai
電話番号案内

engaged
o·hanashichū
お話し中

extension
naisen
内線

number
ban·gō
番号

operator
kōkanshu
交換手

phone (*verb*)
denwa shimas
電話します

phone box
denwa bok·ks
電話ボックス

telephone
denwa
電話

telephone directory
denwa ban·gōchō
電話番号帳

is there a phone round here?
chikak ni denwa ga arimas ka?

近くに電話がありますか？

can I use your phone?
denwa o karite ī des ka?

電話を借りていいですか？

I'd like to make a phone call to Britain
Eikoku e denwa shtai des

英国へ電話したいです

I want to reverse the charges
uketori·nin barai ni shtai des

受取人払いにしたいです

hello
moshi moshi

もしもし

TELEPHONING

could I speak to Yoko?
Yōko·san o onegai shimas

ようこさんをお願
いします

hello, this is Simon speaking
moshi moshi, Saimon des

もしもし、サイモ
ンです

can I leave a message?
den·gon o onegai shimas

伝言をお願いします

do you speak English?
Eigo ga wakarimas ka?

英語 がわかりま
すか？

could you say that again very very slowly?
totemo yuk·kri, mō ichido it·te kudasai

とてもゆっくり、
もう一度言ってく
ださい

could you tell him Jim called?
Jimu ga denwa shta to tstaete kudasai

ジムが電話した
と伝えてください

could you ask her to ring me back?
watashi ni denwa sru yō, tstaete kudasai

私に電話するよう
伝えてください

I'll call back later
ato de kake·naoshimas

後でかけなおします

my number is ...
kochira no denwa ban·gō wa ... des

こちらの電話番号
は・・・です

76 32 11
nana rok san ni ichi ichi

七六三二一一

TELEPHONING

just a minute please
shōshō omachi kudasai

少々お待ちください

he's not in
kare wa ima imasen

彼は今いません

sorry, I've got the wrong number
sumimasen, machigai denwa des

すみません、間違い電話です

it's a terrible line
hidoi kaisen des

ひどい回線です

REPLIES

ちょっと待ってください

chot·to mat·te kudasai
hang on

どなたですか？

donata des ka?
who's calling?

長距離電話	chōkyori denwa **long-distance call**	内線	naisen **extension**
電話帳	denwa·chō **directory**	市外電話	shigai denwa **out-of-town call**
電話料金	denwa ryōkin **call charge**	市内電話	shinai denwa **local call**
国際電話	koksai denwa **international call**	テレホンカード	terehon kādo **phonecard**
公衆電話	kōshū denwa **public telephone**	１１９番	119 **ambulance, fire brigade**
		１１０番	110 **police**

NUMBERS, THE DATE, THE TIME

0 zero	ゼロ	**16** jū rok	十六
1 ichi	一	**17** jū shichi	十七
2 ni	二	**18** jū hachi	十八
3 san	三	**19** jū kyū	十九
4 shi	四	**20** ni jū	二十
5 go	五	**21** ni jū ichi	二十一
6 rok	六	**22** ni jū ni	二十二
7 shichi	七	**30** san jū	三十
8 hachi	八	**35** san jū go	三十五
9 kyū	九	**40** yon jū	四十
10 jū	十	**50** go jū	五十
11 jū ichi	十一	**60** rok jū	六十
12 jū ni	十二	**70** shichi jū	七十
13 jū san	十三	**80** hachi jū	八十
14 jū shi	十四	**90** kyū jū	九十
15 jū go	十五	**91** kyū jū ichi	九十一

NUMBERS, THE DATE, THE TIME

100 hyak	百	**2,000** ni sen	二千
101 hyak ichi	百一	**10,000** ichi man	一万
200 ni hyak	二百	**1,000,000** hyak man	百万
202 ni hyak ni	二百二	**100,000,000** ichi oku	一億
1,000 sen	千		

1st (*date*) tsuitach	一日	**6th** muika	六日
2nd ftsuka	二日	**7th** nanuka	七日
3rd mik·ka	三日	**8th** yōka	八日
4th yok·ka	四日	**9th** kokonoka	九日
5th itska	五日	**10th** tōka	十日

what's the date?
nan·gats nan·nichi des ka? 何月何日ですか？

it's the first of June
rokugats tsuitach des 六月一日です

it's the tenth of May
gogats tōka des 五月十日です

it's the twelfth of May
gogats jū ni nichi des 五月十二日です

1994
sen kyū hyak kyū jū yo
nen 千九百九十四年

what time is it?
ima nanji des ka? 今何時ですか？

NUMBERS, THE DATE, THE TIME

it's midday/midnight
hiru/yonaka des

昼／夜中です

it's one/three o'clock
ichiji/sanji des

一時／三時です

it's twenty past three
sanji nijip·pun sgi des

三時二十分過ぎです

it's twenty to three
sanji nijip·pun mae des

三時二十分前です

it's half past eight
hachiji han des

八時半です

it's a quarter past five
goji jū go fun sgi des

五時十五分過ぎです

it's a quarter to five
goji jū go fun mae des

五時十五分前です

it's six am/six pm
gozen/gogo rokuji des

午前／午後六時です

at two/five p.m.
gogo niji/goji ni

午後二時／五時に

A

a
(*see grammar*)

abacus
soroban
そろばん

about (*approx*)
daitai
大体

above
ue
上

accident
jiko
事故

adaptor
adaptā
アダプター

address
jūsho
住所

aeroplane
hikōki
飛行機

after
ato de
後で

afternoon
gogo
午後

aftershave
aftā·shēb
アフターシェーブ

afterwards
ato de
後で

again
mata
また

against
hantai (no)
反対（の）

age
toshi
年

agent
ējento
エージェント

ago: three days ago
mik·ka mae
三日前

agree: I agree
dōkan des
同感です

AIDS
eidz
エイズ

air
kūki
空気

air-conditioning
eya·kon
エアコン

airmail: by airmail
kōkūbin de
航空便で

airport
kūkō
空港

alarm clock
mezamash·dokei
目覚まし時計

alcohol
arukōru
アルコール

alive
ikite
生きて

all
zembu (no)
全部（の）

all the men/women
otoko/on·na wa mina
男／女は皆

ENGLISH-JAPANESE

allergic to
... ni arerugī (no)
・・・にアレルギー（の）

allowed
yurusarete
許されて

all right: that's all right
daijōbu des
大丈夫です

almost
hotondo
ほとんど

alone
hitori de
ひとりで

also
mo
も

always
itsmo
いつも

a.m.: at 5 a.m.
gozen goji ni
午前五時に

ambulance
kyūkyūsha
救急車

America
Amerika
アメリカ

amp: 13-amp
jūsan ampea
13アンペア

and
soshte
そして

angina
kyōshin·shō
狭心症

angry
okot·te
怒って

animal
dōbuts
動物

another
mō hitots no
もうひとつの

another beer
(*further*)
bīru o mō ip·pai
ビールをもう一杯

another country
(*different*)
bets no kuni
別の国

answer
kotae
答

antibiotic
kōseibus·shitsu
抗生物質

antihistamine
kō·histamin·zai
抗ヒスタミン剤

antiseptic
sak·kinzai
殺菌液

apartment
apāto
アパート

appendicitis
mōchō·en
盲腸炎

apple
rin·go
りんご

appointment
yoyaku
予約

apricot
aprikot·to
アプリコット

April
shigats
四月

area
chīki
地域

arm
ude
腕

arrest
taiho shimas
逮捕します

arrive
tskimas
着きます

art
bijuts
美術

ashtray
haizara
灰皿

ask
tanomimas
たのみます

74

asleep
nemut·te
眠って

aspirin
aspirin
アスピリン

asthma
zensok
ぜんそく

at: at the station
eki de
駅で

at Toyoko's
Toyoko·san no
ie de
とよこさん
の家で

at 3 o'clock
sanji ni
三時に

attractive
miryok·teki (na)
魅力的(な)

aubergine
nas
なす

August
hachigaÌts
八月

aunt
oba·san
(*own*)
oba
おばさん

おば

Australia
Ōstoraria
オースト
ラリア

autumn
aki
秋

awake
okite
起きて

awful
osoroshī
おそろしい

axle
shajik
車軸

B

baby
akachan
赤ちゃん

bachelor
dokshin
独身

back (*of body*)
senaka
背中

at the back of
...
... no ushiro ni
・・・の後に

bad
warui
悪い

bag
kaban
かばん

bag (*suitcase*)
sūtskēs
スーツケ
ース

baggage check
(*US*)
tenimots
azukarisho
手荷物預
かり所

bald
hagete
はげて

ball
bōru
ボール

bamboo shoots
takenoko
竹の子

banana
banana
バナナ

bandage
hōtai
包帯

bank
ginkō
銀行

bar
bā
バー

barber
tokoya
床屋

ENGLISH-JAPANESE

barman
bāten
バーテン

baseball
yakyū
野球

basket
kago
かご

bath
ofuro
お風呂

bathroom
ofuroba
お風呂場

battery
kandenchi
乾電池
(for car)
bat·terī
バッテリー

be
(see grammar)

beach
hama
浜

beans
mame
豆

beard
hige
髭

beautiful
utskushī
美しい

because
nazenara
なぜなら

bed
bed·do
ベッド

bedroom
shinshits
寝室

beef
gyūnik
牛肉

beer
bīru
ビール

before
mae ni
前に

begin
hajimemas
始めます

beginning
hajimari
始まり

behind
ushiro
後

Belgium
Berugī
ベルギー

bell
beru
ベル
(for door)
yobirin
呼び鈴

below
shta (no)
下（の）

belt
beruto
ベルト

bend
kābu
カーブ

best: the best
saikō (no)
最高（の）

better
mot·to ī
もっといい

between
aida (no)
間（の）

bicycle
jitensha
自転車

big
ōkī
大きい

bill
okanjō
お勘定

bird
tori
鳥

biro *(R)*
bōru·pen
ボールペン

birthday
tanjōbi
誕生日

biscuit
bisket·to
ビスケット

bit: a little bit
skoshi bakari
少しばかり

bite *(insect)*
sashimas
刺します

black
kuro
黒

76

ENGLISH-JAPANESE

blanket
mōhu
毛布

bleed
shuk·kets
shimas
出血します

blind
mōjin
盲人

blocked
tsumat·te
つまって

blond
kimpats
金髪

blood
ketsu·eki
血液

blouse
buraus
ブラウス

blue
aoi
青い

boat
bōto
ボート

body
karada
体

bomb
bakudan
爆弾

bone
hone
骨

book
hon
本

bookshop
hon·ya
本屋

boot (*shoe*)
būts
ブーツ

(*car*)
torank
トランク

border
kok·kyō
国境

boring
taikutsu (na)
退屈（な）

born: I was born in 1963
watashi wa 1963
nen umare des
私は1963年
生まれです

boss
bos
ボス

both: both of them
ryōhō tomo
両方とも

bottle
bin
びん

bottle-opener
sen·nuki
栓抜き

bowl
chawan
茶わん

box
hako
箱

boy
otoko no ko
男の子

boyfriend
bōifrendo
ボーイフ
レンド

bra
brajā
ブラジャー

bracelet
udewa
腕輪

brake
burēki
ブレーキ

brandy
burandē
ブランデ
ィー

brave
yūkan (na)
勇敢（な）

bread
pan
パン

break
kowashimas
壊します

breakfast
chōshok
朝食

bridge (*over river etc*)
hashi — 橋

briefcase
burīfu·kēs — ブリーフケース

bring
mot·te kimas — 持ってきます

Britain
Eikok — 英国

broken
kowarete — 壊れて

brooch
burōchi — ブローチ

brother (*older: own*)
ani — 兄
(*older: someone else's*)
onī·san — お兄さん
(*younger: own*)
otōto — 弟
(*younger: someone else's*)
otōto·san — 弟さん

brown
cha·iro — 茶色

brush
burash — ブラシ

bucket
bakets — バケツ

Buddha
hotoke·sama — 仏様

building
biru — ビル

bulb (*light*)
denkyū — 電球

burn
yakimas — 焼きます

bus
bas — バス

business
shigoto — 仕事

businessman
bijines·man — ビジネスマン

business trip
shut·chō — 出張

business woman
bijines ūman — ビジネスウーマン

bus station
bas no tāminaru — バスのターミナル

bus stop
bas·tei — バス停

but
demo — でも

butter
batā — バター

button
botan — ボタン

buy
kaimas — 買います

by
... de — ・・・で

by car
kruma de — 車で

C

café
kis·saten — 喫茶店

cake
kēki — ケーキ

calculator
keisanki — 計算機

ENGLISH-JAPANESE

calendar
karendā
カレンダー

camera (*still*)
kamera
カメラ

(*movie*)
satsueiki
撮影機

can (*tin*)
kanzume
缶詰

**can: can I/she
...?** (*permission*)
...te ī des ka?
(*see grammar*)
・・・ーてい
いですか？

Canada
Kanada
カナダ

cancel
tori·keshimas
取り消し
ます

car
kruma
車

**card: business
card**
meishi
名刺

**careful: be
careful!**
ki o tskete
気をつけて

car park
chūshajō
駐車場

carpet
jūtan
じゅうたん

carrot
ninjin
人参

cassette
kaset·to
カセット

cassette player
kaset·to
rekōdā
カセットレ
コーダー

cat
neko
猫

cauliflower
karifurawā
カリフラ
ワー

cave
hora·ana
洞穴

ceiling
tenjō
天井

centigrade
ses·shi
摂氏

central heating
sentoraru
hīting·g
セントラル
ヒーティング

centre
chūshin
中心

century
seiki
世紀

certificate
shōmeisho
証明書

chain
ksari
鎖

chair
is
椅子

change (*small*)
kozeni
小銭

change (trains)
norikaemas
乗り換えます

character
(*Chinese*)
kanji
漢字

cheap
yasui
安い

check (*verb*)
tenken shimas
点検します

cheers! (*toast*)
kampai!
乾杯！

cheese
chīz
チーズ

chemist
ksuri·ya
薬屋

ENGLISH-JAPANESE

cheque
kogit·te 小切手

cherry
sakurambo さくらんぼ

chest
mune 胸

chewing gum
chūin·gam チューインガム

chicken
niwatori 鶏

child
kodomo 子供

chin
ago 顎

China
Chūgok 中国

chips
frenchi·frai フレンチフライ

chocolate
chokorēto チョコレート

Christmas
kurismas クリスマス

church
kyōkai 教会

cigar
hamaki 葉巻

cigarette
tabako タバコ

cinema
eigakan 映画館

city centre
shinai 市内

clean (*adjective*)
kirei (na) きれい（な）

clean (*verb*)
seisō shimas 清掃します

clever
kashkoi 賢い

clock
tokei 時計

close (*verb*)
shimemas 閉めます

closed
shimat·te 閉まって

closet (*US*)
todana 戸棚

clothes
yōfuku 洋服

clothes peg
sentaku·basami 洗濯挟み

cloudy
kumori (no) 曇り（の）

coat
kōto コート

coathanger
han·gā ハンガー

cockroach
gokiburi ゴキブリ

coffee
kōhī コーヒー

cold
tsmetai 冷たい

I've got a cold
kaze o
hikimashta 風邪をひきました

colour
iro 色

colour film
karā firum カラーフィルム

comb
kushi 櫛

come
kimas 来ます

ENGLISH-JAPANESE

come back
modorimas — 戻ります

come in!
dōzo — どうぞ

comfortable
kaiteki (na) — 快適（な）

comic (book)
man·ga — 漫画

company
kaisha — 会社

complicated
fkuzatsu (na) — 複雑（な）

computer
kompyūtā — コンピューター

concert
konsāto — コンサート

condom
kondōm — コンドーム

congratulations!
omedetō! — おめでとう!

constipated
benpi (no) — 便秘（の）

consulate
ryōjikan — 領事館

contact lenses
kontakto renz — コンタクトレンズ

cool
suzushī — 涼しい

corkscrew
koruk·nuki — コルク抜き

corner
kado — 角

correct
tadashī — 正しい

cotton
momen — 木綿

cotton wool
das·shimen — 脱脂綿

cough
seki — 咳

country
kuni — 国

course: of course
mochiron — もちろん

crab
kani — 蟹

cream
kurīm — クリーム

credit card
kurejit·to kādo — クレジットカード

crowded
konde — 混んで

cry
nakimas — 泣きます

cucumber
kyūri — きゅうり

cup
kap·pu — カップ

cupboard
todana — 戸棚

curtain
kāten — カーテン

custom
shūkan — 習慣

customs
zeikan — 税関

cyclist
saikristo — サイクリスト

ENGLISH-JAPANESE

D

damp shimet·te	湿って	
dangerous abunai	危ない	
dark kurai	暗い	
date (*time*) hizuke	日付	
daughter ojō·san	お嬢さん	
(*own*) musume	娘	
day hi	日	
the day before yesterday ototoi	おととい	
the day after tomorrow asat·te	あさって	
dead shinde	死んで	
deaf mimi ga tōi	耳が遠い	
death shi	死	
decaffeinated kafein nuki (no)	カフェイン 抜き（の）	
December jūnigats	十二月	
deep fukai	深い	
delicious oishī	おいしい	

dentist ha·isha	歯医者	
deodorant deodoranto	デオドラント	
depend: it depends ba·ai ni yorimas	場合に よります	
dessert dezāto	デザート	
diabetic tōnyōbyō	糖尿病	
dialect hōgen	方言	
dialling code shigai·kyokuban	市外局番	
diamond daiyamondo	ダイヤモンド	
diarrhoea geri	下痢	
diary nik·ki	日記	
(*planner*) techō	手帳	
dictionary jisho	辞書	
die shinimas	死にます	
different chigat·te	違って	
difficult muzukashī	難しい	
dining room shokdō	食堂	
dinner yūshok	夕食	
direct choksets (no)	直接（の）	
direction hōkō	方向	

ENGLISH-JAPANESE

dirty
kitanai
汚い

disabled
shintai shōgai
身体障害

disaster
saigai
災害

disco
disko
ディスコ

disease
byōki
病気

disgusting
iya (na)
いや（な）

disinfectant
shōdokzai
消毒剤

distance
kyori
距離

district (*in town*)
chiku
地区

disturb
jama shimas
邪魔します

divorced
rikonshte
離婚して

do
shimas
します

that'll do nicely
sore de ī des
それで
いいです

doctor
oisha·san
お医者さん

dog
inu
犬

doll
nin·gyō
人形

dollar
doru
ドル

door
doa
ドア

down: down there
asoko
あそこ

downstairs
shta
下

dream
yume
夢

dress
dores
ドレス

drink
nomimono
飲み物

drink (*verb*)
nomimas
飲みます

drinking water
inryōsui
飲料水

drive
unten shimas
運転します

driver
unten·shu
運転手

it's the other driver's fault
ano hito no sei des
あの人のせいです

driving licence
unten·menkyoshō
運転免許証

drugstore
ksuri·ya
薬屋

drunk
yop·parai (no)
酔っ払い（の）

dry
kawaite
乾いて

dry-cleaner
dorai·kurīningu·ya
ドライクリーニング屋

duck
ahiru
あひる

83

ENGLISH-JAPANESE

E

ear
mimi
耳

early
hayai
早い

earrings
iyaring·g
イヤリング

earth (*soil*)
tsuchi
土

east
higashi
東

easy
yasashī
やさしい

eat
tabemas
食べます

egg
tamago
卵

boiled egg
yude tamago
ゆで卵

either . . . or . . .
. . . ka . . . ka
・・・か
・・・か

elastic
shinshuksei (no)
伸縮性（の）

elbow
hiji
肘

electric
denki (no)
電気（の）

electricity
denki
電気

electronics
erekutoronikus
エレクト
ロニクス

elevator
erebētā
エレベー
ター

else: something else
hoka no mono
他のもの

embassy
taishkan
大使館

emergency
hijō
非常

Emperor of Japan
Ten·nō Heika
天皇陛下

empty
kara (no)
空（の）

end
owari
終わり

engaged (*toilet*)
shiyōchū
使用中
(*to be married*)
kon·yakshte
婚約して

engine
enjin
エンジン

England
Igiris
イギリス

English (*adjective*)
Igiris (no)
イギリス（の）
(*language*)
Eigo
英語

English girl/woman
Igiris·jin
イギリス人

Englishman
Igiris·jin
イギリス人

enough
jūbun
充分

that's enough
mō ī des
もういいです

entrance
iriguchi
入り口
(*to house*)
genkan
玄関

envelope
fūtō
封筒

ENGLISH-JAPANESE

epileptic
tenkan (no) — 癲癇（の）

Europe
Yōrop·pa — ヨーロッパ

evening
yūgata — 夕方

every
subete no — すべての

everyone
min·na — 皆

everything
subete — すべて

excellent
subarashī — すばらしい

exchange
ryōgae shimas — 両替します

exchange rate
ryōgae rēto — 両替レート

exhibition
tenrankai — 展覧会

exit
deguchi — 出口

expensive
takai — 高い

explain
setsmei shimas — 説明します

eye
me — 目

eye shadow
ai·shadō — アイシャドー

F

face
ka·o — 顔

face mask (*for colds*)
masku — マスク

factory
kōjō — 工場

family
kazok — 家族

fan (*mechanical*)
sempūki — 扇風機

far (away)
tōi — 遠い

fast
hayai — 早い

fat (*person*)
futot·te — 太って

father
otō·san — お父さん
(*own*)
chichi — 父

faucet (*US*)
jaguchi — 蛇口

faulty
kek·kan (no) — 欠陥（の）

favourite
ichiban ski (na) — 一番好き（な）

February
nigats — 二月

feel: I feel well/unwell
kibun ga ī/warui des — 気分がいい／悪いです

ferry
ferī — フェリー

fever
nets — 熱

few: a few
ikutska — いくつか

field
nohara — 野原

filling (*tooth*)
ha no tsumemono — 歯の詰め物

ENGLISH-JAPANESE

film (*for camera*)
firum フィルム
(*at cinema*)
eiga 映画

find
mitskemas 見付けます

finger
yubi 指

finish
owarimas 終わります

fire
kaji 火事
(*blaze*)
hono·o 炎

fire extinguisher
shōkaki 消火器

first
saisho (no) 最初（の）

first aid
ōkyū teate 応急手当て

first class
it·tō 一等

fish
sakana 魚

fit (*healthy*)
jōbu (na) 丈夫（な）

fizzy
tansan (no) 炭酸（の）

flash
furash フラッシュ

flat
apāto アパート

flat (*adjective*)
taira (na) 平ら（な）

flavour
aji 味

flea
nomi 蚤

flight
hikōbin 飛行便

floor (*of room*)
yuka 床
(*storey*)
kai 階

flour
komugiko 小麦粉

flower
hana 花

flu
ryūkan 流感

fly
hae ハエ

fly (*verb*)
tobimas 飛びます

folk music
minzoku on·gak 民族音楽

follow
tsuite ikimas ついていきます

food
tabemono 食物

food poisoning
shokchūdoku 食中毒

foot
ashi 足
on foot
aruite 歩いて

football (*soccer*)
sak·kā サッカー

for
... no tame ni ・・・のために

forbidden
kinjirarete 禁じられて

foreigner
gaikoku·jin 外国人

forest
mori 森

86

forget
wasuremas 忘れます

fork
fōku フォーク
(in road)
sansaro 三叉路

form
yōshi 用紙

fortnight
nishūkan 二週間

forward (mail)
atesaki 宛先

France
Frans フランス

free
hima (na) 暇（な）
(of charge)
tada ただ

French (adjective)
Frans no フランス（の）

French fries
frenchi·frai フレンチフライ

Friday
kin·yōbi 金曜日

fridge
reizōko 冷蔵庫

friend
tomodachi 友達

from: from Tokyo to Osaka 東京から大阪まで
Tōkyō kara Ōsaka made

front (part)
mae 前
in front of ...
... no mae ni ・・・の前に

fruit
kudamono 果物

Fuji: Mount Fuji
Fujisan 富士山

full
ip·pai 一杯

fun: have fun!
tanoshinde kudasai! 楽しんでください！

funny (strange)
okashī おかしい
(amusing)
omoshiroi 面白い

furniture
kagu 家具

further
mot·to tōi もっと遠い

fuse
hyūz ヒューズ

G

garage (repair)
shūrikōjō 修理工場

garden
niwa 庭

garlic
nin·nik にんにく

gas (US: for car)
gasorin ガソリン

gate (airport)
gēto ゲート

gay
homo (no) ホモ（の）

gear
giya ギヤ

gents (toilet)
danseiyō 男性用

genuine
hom·mono 本物

Germany
Doits — ドイツ

get (*obtain*)
te ni iremas — 手に入れます

can you tell me how to get to ...?
... e wa dō iku ka oshiete kudasai — ...へは どう行くか 教えてくだ さい

get back (*return*)
modorimas — 戻ります

get off
orimas — 降ります

get up
okimas — 起きます

gin
jin — ジン

girl
on·na no ko — 女の子

girlfriend
gārufrendo — ガールフ レンド

give
agemas — 上げます

give back
modoshimas — 戻します

glad
ureshī — 嬉しい

glass (*for drinking*)
kop·pu — コップ

glasses
megane — 眼鏡

gloves
tebukuro — 手袋

glue
nori — 糊

go
ikimas — 行きます

go in
hairimas — 入ります

go out
demas — 出ます

go down
shta e ikimas — 下へ行きます

go up
ue e ikimas — 上へ行きます

go through
tōri·nukemas — 通り抜けます

go away
mukō e ikimas — 向こうへ行 きます

God
kami sama — 神様

gold
kin — 金

good
ī — いい

good!
yokat·ta ! — よかった！

goodbye
sayōnara — さようなら

got: have you got ...?
... ga arimas ka? — ...があ りますか？

government
seifu — 政府

grandfather
ojī·san — おじいさん
(*own*)
sofu — 祖父

grandmother
obā·san — おばあさん
(*own*)
sobo — 祖母

grapefruit
gurēp·furūts — グレープ フルーツ

grapes budō	ぶどう	**hairdresser** biyōin	美容院
grass ksa	草	**half** hambun	半分
grateful kansha (no)	感謝（の）	**half an hour** hanjikan	半時間
green midori·iro	緑色	**ham** hamu	ハム
grey hai·iro	灰色	**hammer** kanazuchi	金槌
grocer shokuryōhinten	食料品店	**hand** te	手
ground floor ik·kai	一階	**handbag** handobag·g	ハンドバッグ
group gurūp	グループ	**handkerchief** hankachi	ハンカチ
guarantee hoshō	保証	**handle** handoru	ハンドル
guest okyak·san	お客さん	**hand luggage** tenimots	手荷物
guide gaido	ガイド	**handsome** hansam (na)	ハンサム（な）
guidebook gaido buk·k	ガイドブック	**happy** ureshī	嬉しい
guitar gitā	ギター	**happy New Year!** akemashte omedetō gozaimas	明けまして おめでとう ございます
gun (*pistol*) pistoru (*rifle*) jū	ピストル 銃	**harbour** minato	港
		hard katai (*difficult*) muzukashī	堅い 難しい
H		**hat** bōshi	帽子
hair kami	髪	**hate** nikumimas	憎みます
haircut (*for men*) sampats (*for women*) kat·to	散髪 カット		

have
mochimas 持ちます

I have an umbrella
kasa o mot·te imas 傘を持っています

do you have a ...?
... o mot·te imas ka? ・・・を持っていますか？

do you have ...? (*shopping*)
... ga arimas ka? ・・・がありますか？

I have to ...
...anakereba narimasen; (*see grammar*) ・・・あなーければなりません

hay fever
kafumbyō 花粉病

he
kare; (*see grammar*) 彼

head
atama 頭

headache
zutsū 頭痛

headlights
hed·do raito ヘッドライト

health
kenkō 健康

hear
kikimas 聞きます

hearing aid
hochōki 補聴器

heart
shinzō 心臓

heart attack
shinzō mahi 心臓マヒ

heat
atsusa 暑さ

heating
dambō 暖房

heavy
omoi 重い

heel
kakato かかと

helicopter
herikoptā ヘリコプター

hello
kon·nichi wa! こんにちわ

help: thanks for your help
tetsdat·te krete arigatō 手伝ってくれてありがとう

help (*verb*)
tetsdaimas 手伝います

help!
taskete! 助けて

her (*possessive*)
kanojo no (*object*) kanojo o; (*see grammar*) 彼女の 彼女を

herbs (*cooking*)
hāb ハーブ

here
koko ここ

hers
kanojo no; (*see grammar*) 彼女のです

hiccups
shak·kuri しゃっくり

high
takai 高い

hill
oka 丘

him
kare o; (*see grammar*) 彼を

hip
oshiri — お尻

hire
karimas — 借ります

his
kare no; (see
grammar) — 彼の

hit
nagurimas — 殴ります

hitchhike
hit·ch haiku
shimas — ヒッチハイ
クします

hole
ana — 穴

holiday
yasumi — 休み
(public)
saijitsu — 祭日

home: at home
uchi de — うちで
(in my country)
watashi no kuni
de — 私の国で
go home
kaerimas — 帰ります

honey
hachimits — 蜂蜜

hope
kibō — 希望

horrible
osoroshī — おそろしい

horse
uma — 馬

hospital
byōin — 病院

hospitality
motenashi — もてなし

hot
atsui — 暑い
(to taste)
karai — からい

hotel
hoteru — ホテル

hour
jikan — 時間

house
ie — 家

how?
dōshte? — どうして？

how are you?
ogenki des ka ? — お元気で
すか？

how are things?
ikaga osugoshi
des ka? — いかがお過
ごしですか？

how many?
ikuts (no)? — いくつ
（の）？

how much?
(price)
ikra des ka? — いくらで
すか？

**hungry: I'm
hungry**
onaka ga suite
imas — おなかが空
いています

hurry: hurry up!
isoide! — 急いで

hurt
itamimas — 痛みます

husband (own)
shujin — 主人
(someone else's)
goshujin — 御主人

ENGLISH-JAPANESE

I

I
watashi; (see grammar) — 私

ice
kōri — 氷

ice cream
ais·kurīm — アイスクリーム

idiot
hakchi — 白痴

if
moshi — もし

ill
byōki (no) — 病気（の）

immediately
sugu — すぐ

important
taisetsu (na) — 大切（な）

impossible
fukanō (na) — 不可能（な）

in: in English
Eigo de — 英語で

is he in?
kare wa imas ka? — 彼はいますか？

in Nagoya
Nagoya ni/de; (see grammar) — 名古屋に／で

included
... komi — ・・・込み

indigestion
shōka furyō — 消化不良

industry
san·gyō — 産業

infection
kansen — 感染

information
jōhō — 情報

injured
kega o shte — 怪我をして

innocent
mujaki (na) — 無邪気（な）

insect
mushi — 虫

insect repellent
mushiyoke — 虫除け

insurance
hoken — 保険

intelligent
sōmei (na) — 聡明（な）

interesting
omoshiroi — 面白い

invitation
shōtai — 招待

Ireland
Airurando — アイルランド

iron (metal)
tetsu — 鉄
(for clothes)
airon — アイロン

ironmonger
kanamono·ya — 金物屋

island
shima — 島

it: it is ...
... des; (see grammar) — ・・・です

J

jack (car)
jak·ki — ジャッキ

jacket
jaket·to — ジャケット

ENGLISH-JAPANESE

January
ichigats
一月

Japan
Nihon
日本

Japanese
(*adjective*)
Nihon (no)
日本の
(*language*)
Nihon·go
日本語
(*person*)
Nihon·jin
日本人

Japanese-style
wahū
和風

jaw
ago
顎

jazz
jaz
ジャズ

jeans
jīnz
ジーンズ

jewellery
hōseki
宝石

job
shigoto
仕事

joke
jōdan
冗談

journey
ryokō
旅行

jug
mizusashi
水差し

juice
jūs
ジュース

July
shchigats
七月

junction (*road*)
kōsaten
交差点

June
rokugats
六月

just: just two
futats dake
二つだけ

K

key
kagi
鍵

kidneys
jinzō
腎臓

kilo
kiro
キロ

kilometre
kiromētoru
キロメートル

kind
shinsets (na)
親切（な）

kiss
kis
キス

kiss (*verb*)
kis shimas
キスします

kitchen
daidokoro
台所

knee
hiza
ひざ

knife
naifu
ナイフ

know
shit·te imas
知っています

I don't know
shirimasen
知りません

Korea
Kankok
韓国
North Korea
Kita·chōsen
北朝鮮
South Korea
Minami·chōsen
南朝鮮

ENGLISH-JAPANESE

L

lacquer ware shik·ki	漆器	**lawn** shibafu	芝生
ladder hashigo	ハシゴ	**lawyer** ben·goshi	弁護士
ladies (room) keshōshits	化粧室	**laxative** gezai	下剤
lady fujin	婦人	**lazy** namakemono (no)	なまけもの（の）
lake mizu·umi	湖	**leaflet** chirashi	チラシ
lamb kohitsuji	小羊	**leak** more	漏れ
lamp stando	スタンド	**learn** manabimas	学びます
language gen·go	言語	**leather** kawa	皮
large ōki	大きい	**leave** okimas	置きます
last saigo (no)	最後（の）	(train etc) tachimas	発ちます
last year kyonen	去年	(forget) oki·wasuremas	置き忘れます
late osoi	遅い	**left** hidari	左
		on the left (of) (... no) hidari ni	（・・・の）左に
laugh waraimas	笑います	**left-handed** hidari kiki (no)	左利き（の）
launderette koin·randorī	コインランドリー	**left luggage** tenimotsu azukarisho	手荷物預かり所
laundry (to wash) sentakmono	洗濯物	**leg** ashi	脚
(place) sentakuya	洗濯屋	**lemon** remon	レモン
law hōrits	法律	**lemonade** saidā	サイダー

ENGLISH-JAPANESE

lemon tea
remon tī
レモンティー

lens
renz
レンズ

less than . . .
. . . ika
・・・以下

lesson
jugyō
授業

letter (*in mail*)
tegami
手紙

letterbox
tegami·uke
手紙受け

library
toshokan
図書館

licence
menkyo
免許

lid
futa
蓋

lie down
yoko ni narimas
横になります

lift (*elevator*)
erebētā
エレベーター

light (*in room*)
denki
電気
(*on car*)
raito
ライト

have you got a light?
mat·chi o mot·te imas ka?
マッチを持っていますか？

light (*adjective*)
karui
軽い

light bulb
denkyū
電球

lighter
raitā
ライター

like
ski des
好きです

I like . . .
. . . ga ski des
・・・が好きです

I would like a . . .
. . .ga hoshī des
・・・が欲しいです

I'd like to . . .
. . .·tai des; (*see grammar*)
・・・たいです

like (*as*)
. . . no yō
・・・のよう

lip
kuchibiru
唇

lipstick
kuchibeni
口紅

liqueur
rikyūru
リキュール

listen (to)
(. . .) o kikimas
（・・・を）聞きます

litre
rit·toru
リットル

little
chīsai
小さい

a little bit (of)
(. . . o) skoshi dake
（・・・を）少しだけ

live
ikimas
生きます
(*in town etc*)
sumimas
住みます

liver
kanzō
肝臓

living room
ima
居間

lock
kagi
鍵

lock (*verb*)
kagi o kakemas
鍵を掛けます

95

long
nagai 長い

a long time
nagai aida 長い間

look (*seem*)
miemas 見えます

look (at)
(... o) mimas (・・・を)見ます

look for
sagashimas 捜します

look like
nite imas 似ています

look out!
ki o tskete! 気をつけて

lorry
torak·ku トラック

lose
nakushimas なくします

lost property office
ishits·butsu tori·atskaijo 遺失物取り扱い所

lot: a lot (of)
(... ga) taksan (・・・が)たくさん

loud
sawagashī 騒がしい

love
ai 愛

love (*verb*)
aishimas 愛します

lovely
steki (na) 素敵（な）

low (*prices*)
yasui 安い

(*height*)
hikui 低い

luck
un 運

good luck!
kō un o inorimas 好運を祈ります

luggage
nimots 荷物

lunch
chūshok 昼食

lungs
hai 肺

M

mad
kichigai (no) 気違い（の）

magazine
zas·shi 雑誌

mail
yūbim·butsu 郵便物

make
tskurimas 作ります

made in Japan
Nihonsei (no) 日本製（の）

make-up
keshō 化粧

man
otoko no hito 男の人

manager
manējā マネージャー

many
taksan (no) たくさん（の）

many ...
... ga taksan ・・・がたくさん

map
chiz 地図

ENGLISH-JAPANESE

March
san·gats 三月

market
ichiba 市場

married
kikon (no) 既婚（の）

martial arts
budō 武道

mascara
maskara マスカラ

mat
tatami 畳

match (*light*)
mat·chi マッチ
(*sport*)
shiai 試合

material (*cloth*)
nunoji 布地

matter: it doesn't matter
dō demo ī des どうでもいいです

mattress
mat·tores マットレス

May
gogats 五月

maybe
sō kamo shiremasen そうかも知れません

mayonnaise
mayonēz マヨネーズ

me
watashi 私
me too
watashi mo; (*see grammar*) 私も

meal
shokuji 食事

measles
hashka はしか

meat
niku 肉

medicine (*drug*)
ksuri 薬

meeting
kaigi 会議

melon
meron メロン

mend
shūri shimas 修理します

men's room (*US*)
dansei·yō 男性用

menu
menyū メニュー

message
den·gon 伝言

metal
kinzok 金属

metre
mētoru メートル

middle
man·naka (no) 真ん中（の）

milk
miruk ミルク

mine
watashi no mono; (*see grammar*) 私のもの

mineral water
mineraru uōtā ミネラルウォーター

minute
fun 分

mirror
kagami 鏡

Miss
. . . san ・・・さん

miss (*train etc*)
nori·okuremas 乗り遅れます

97

ENGLISH-JAPANESE

I miss you
anata ga inakte
sabishī des
あなたが
いなくて淋し
いです

mistake
machigai
間違い

modern
modan (na)
モダン（な）

Monday
getsyōbi
月曜日

money
okane
お金

month
tski
月

moon
tski
月

moped
tansha
単車

more
mot·to
もっと
no more ...
... wa mō
taksan
・・・はもう
たくさん

morning
asa
朝

mosquito
ka
蚊

most (of)
(... no hotondo
(・・・の)
ほとんど

mother
okā·san
お母さん
(*own*)
haha
母

motorbike
ōtobai
オートバイ

motorway
kōsok·dōro
高速道路

mountain
yama
山

mouse
nezumi
鼠

moustache
kuchi·hige
口髭

mouth
kuchi
口

movie
eiga
映画

movie theater
(*US*)
eigakan
映画館

Mr
...san
・・・さん

Mrs
...san
・・・さん

Ms
...san
・・・さん

much
taksan (no)
たくさん（の）

muscle
kin·nik
筋肉

museum
hakubutskan
博物館

mushroom
mas·shurūm
マッシュ
ルーム

music
on·gak
音楽

must: I/she must
...anakereba
narimasen; (*see
grammar*)
・・・-あな
ければなりま
せん

mustard
karashi
からし

my
watashi no; (*see
grammar*)
私の

ENGLISH-JAPANESE

N

nail (*in wall etc*) kugi	釘	**the nearest . . .** ichiban chikai . . .	一番近い
nail clippers tsme·kiri	爪きり	**necessary** hitsyō (na)	必要（な）
nailfile tsme yasuri	爪やすり	**neck** kubi	首
nail polish manikyua	マニキュア	**necklace** nek·kures	ネックレス
nail polish remover jokō·eki	除光液	**need: I need . . .** watashi wa . . . ga hitsyō des	私は・・・が必要です
name namae	名前	**needle** hari	針
what's your name? o·namae wa nan to os·shaimas ka?	お名前は何とおっしゃいますか？	**negative** (*film*) nega	ネガ
my name is Jim watashi no namae wa Jim des	私の名前はジムです	**nervous** shinkei·shits (na)	神経質（な）
		never ·masen; (*see grammar*)	ーません
napkin napkin	ナプキン	**new** atarashī	新しい
nappy omuts	おむつ	**new** (*brand-new*) atarashī	新しい
narrow semai	狭い	**news** nyūs	ニュース
nationality kokseki	国籍	**newspaper** shimbun	新聞
natural shizen (na)	自然（な）	**New Year** ·shōgats	正月
near . . . . . . no chikaku	・・・の近く	**next** tonari (no) (*following*) tsgi (no)	隣（の） 次（の）
near here koko no chikaku	ここの近く	**next to** . . . no tonari ni	・・・の隣に

nice
ī いい
(*food*)
oishī おいしい

night
yoru 夜

nightdress
nemaki 寝巻

no
īe いいえ
no ...
... wa ・・・はあり
arimasen; (*see* ません
grammar)

nobody
dare mo 誰も・・・
...masen; (*see* -ません
grammar)

noise
sō·on 騒音

noisy
urusai うるさい

non-smoking
kin·en (no) 禁煙（の）

normal
seijō (na) 正常（な）

north
kita 北

nose
hana 鼻

not
·masen; (*see* -ません
grammar)

notebook
techō 手帳

nothing
nani mo 何も・・・
...masen; (*see* -ません
grammar)

November
jūichigats 十一月

now
ima 今

number
kazu 数

nurse
kangofu 看護婦

O

October
jūgats 十月

of
... no; (*see* ・・・の
grammar)

office
jimusho 事務所

often
yok よく

oil
oiru オイル

OK
ōkē オーケー
I'm OK
watashi wa 私は大丈
daijōbu des 夫です

old (*person*)
toshiyori (no) 年寄（の）
(*thing*)
furui 古い

**how old are
you?**
nansai des ka? 何才です
か？

I'm 25 years old
nijūgosai des 二十五才
です

100

ENGLISH-JAPANESE

omelette
omurets — オムレツ

on
. . . no ue ni — ・・・の上に

one
hitots — ひとつ

onion
tamanegi — 玉葱

only
tat·ta — たった

open (*adjective*)
hiraite — 開いて

open (*verb*)
akimas — 開きます

opera
opera — オペラ

operation
shujuts — 手術

opposite
hantai (no) — 反対（の）

optician
megane·ya — 眼鏡屋

or
mata wa — または

orange
orenji — オレンジ

orange (*colour*)
orenji·iro — オレンジ色

orchestra
ōkestora — オーケストラ

Oriental
Tōyō (no) — 東洋（の）

other
hoka no — 他の

our(s)
watashtachi no;
(*see grammar*) — 私達の

out: she's out
kanojo wa
gaishutsu·chū
des — 彼女は外出中です

outside
soto — 外

over (*above*)
. . . no ue ni — ・・・の上に
(*finished*)
sunde — 済んで

over there
asoko ni — あそこに

oyster
kaki — 牡蠣

P

Pacific Ocean
Taiheiyō — 太平洋

package
kozutsumi — 小包み

packet (*of cigarettes etc*)
hako — 箱

paddy field
suiden — 水田

page
pēji — ページ

pain
itami — 痛み

painful
itai — 痛い

painkiller
itamidome — 痛み止め

painting
e — 絵

palace
kyūden — 宮殿

panties
pantī — パンティー

pants (*trousers*)
zubon — ズボン

paper
kami — 紙

parcel
kozutsmi — 小包み

pardon?
nan to īmashta ka? — 何と言いましたか？

parents
goryōshin — 御両親
(*own*)
ryōshin — 両親

park
kōen — 公園

parking lot (*US*)
chūshajō — 駐車場

part
bubun — 部分

party (*celebration*)
pātī — パーティー
(*group*)
dantai — 団体

passport
paspōto — パスポート

path
komichi — 小道

pavement
hodō — 歩道

pay
shiharaimas — 支払います

peach
momo — 桃

peanuts
pīnat·ts — ピーナッツ

pear
nashi — 梨

peas
gurīmpīs — グリーンピース

pedestrian
hokōsha — 歩行者

pen
pen — ペン

pencil
empits — 鉛筆

penicillin
penishirin — ペニシリン

penknife
kogatana — 小刀

people
hito — 人

pepper (*spice*)
koshō — 胡椒
(*red/green*)
pimento/pīman — ピメント／ピーマン
(*chili*)
tōgarashi — 唐辛子

per cent
pāsento — パーセント

perfume
kōsui — 香水

period (*woman's*)
seiri — 生理

person
hito — 人

petrol
gasorin — ガソリン

petrol station
gasorin stando — ガソリンスタンド

phone (*verb*)
denwa o shimas — 電話をします

phone box
denwa bok·ks — 電話ボックス

phonecard
terehon·kādo — テレホンカード

phone number
denwa ban·gō — 電話番号

photograph
shashin — 写真

photograph (*verb*)
shashin o torimas — 写真を撮ります

piece: a piece of
... o hitokire — ・・・を一切れ

pill
piru — ピル

pillow
makura — 枕

pin
pin — ピン

pineapple
painap·puru — パイナップル

pink
pink — ピンク

pipe
suidōkan — 水道管
(*to smoke*)
paip — パイプ

pity: it's a pity
zan·nen des — 残念です

plant
shokubuts — 植物

plastic
puraschik·k — プラスチック

plastic bag
binīru bukuro — ビニール袋

plate
sara — 皿

platform (*station*)
purat·tohōm — プラットホーム

play (*theatre*)
shibai — 芝居

play (*verb: sports*)
shimas — します

pleasant
kimochi no ī — 気持ちのいい

please
onegai shimas — お願いします

pleased
yorokonde — 喜んで

pliers
puraiyā — プライヤー

plug (*electrical*)
purag — プラグ
(*in sink*)
sen — 栓

plum
puram — プラム

p.m.: 3 p.m.
gogo sanji — 午後三時

pocket
poket·to — ポケット

poison
doku — 毒

police
keisats — 警察

policeman
keikan — 警官

ENGLISH-JAPANESE

police station
keisats·sho　警察署
(*small*)
hashutsusho　派出所

polite
teinei (na)　丁寧（な）

politics
seiji　政治

poor (*not rich*)
bimbō (na)　貧乏（な）

pop music
pop·ps　ポップス

pork
butanik　豚肉

possible
kanō (na)　可能（な）

post (*verb*)
tōkan shimas　投函します

postcard
hagaki　葉書

poster
postā　ポスター

post office
yūbin·kyok　郵便局

potato
jaga·imo　ジャガ芋

pound (*money*)
pondo　ポンド

prawn
koebi　小海老

pregnant
ninshin shte　妊娠して

prescription
shohōsen　処方箋

present (*gift*)
prezento　プレゼント

pretty
kirei (na)　きれい（な）

price
nedan　値段

priest (*Christian*)
bokshi　牧師
(*Buddhist*)
obō·san　お坊さん
(*Shinto*)
kan·nushi　神主

prison
keimusho　刑務所

private
kojin (no)　個人（の）

problem
mondai　問題

prohibited
kinjirarete　禁じられて

pronounce
hatsuon shimas　発音します

pull
hikimas　引きます

pump
pomp　ポンプ

puncture
panku　パンク

purple
murasaki　紫

purse (*for money*)
saifu　財布

push
oshimas　押します

pushchair
bebīkā　ベビーカー

put
okimas　置きます

pyjamas
pajama　パジャマ

104

ENGLISH-JAPANESE

Q

quality hinshits	品質
queue gyōrets	行列
quick hayai	早い
quickly hayak	早く
quiet shizka (na)	静か（な）
quite kanari (no)	かなり（の）

R

rabbit usagi	兎
radio rajio	ラジオ
railway tetsdō	鉄道
rain ame	雨
it's raining ame ga fut·te imas	雨が降っています
raincoat rēnkōto	レーンコート
rape fujobōkō	婦女暴行
raspberry razuberī	ラズベリー
rat dobu·nezumi	どぶ鼠

razor higesori	髭剃
razor blade kamisoriba	かみそり刃
read yomimas	読みます
ready yōi ga dekite	用意が出来て
rear lights kōbu raito	後部ライト
receipt ryōshūsho	領収書
reception (*hotel*) uketske	受け付け
record rekōdo	レコード
record player rekōdo purēyā	レコードプレーヤー
red akai	赤い
red·headed akage (no)	赤毛（の）
remember: I remember oboete imas	覚えています
rent (*verb*) karimas	借ります
repair shūzen shimas	修繕します
repeat kuri·kaeshimas	繰り返します
reservation yoyak	予約
rest (*remainder*) nokori	残り
(*sleep*) kyūsok	休息

105

restaurant
restoran — レストラン

restroom (*US*)
toire — トイレ

reverse (*gear*)
bak·k gia — バックギヤ

rheumatism
ryūmachi — リューマチ

rib
abarabone — あばら骨

rice
kome — 米
(*cooked*)
gohan — 御飯

rich
kanemochi (no) — 金持ち（の）

right (*side*)
migi — 右

on the right (of)
(... no) migite ni — (・・・の)
右手に

right (*correct*)
tadashī — 正しい

ring (*on finger*)
yubiwa — 指輪

river
kawa — 川

road
michi — 道

roll
dinā rōru — ディナー
ロール

roof
yane — 屋根

room
heya — 部屋

rope
rōpu — ロープ

rose
bara — バラ

route
rūto — ルート

rubber
gom — ゴム

rubber (*eraser*)
keshigom — 消しゴム

rubber band
wagom — 輪ゴム

rubbish
gomi — ゴミ

rucksack
ryuk·k sak·k — リュック
サック

rude
busahō (na) — 不作法（な）

rug
shkimono — 敷物

ruins
iseki — 遺蹟

rum
ramshu — ラム酒

run
hashirimas — 走ります

S

sad
kanashī — 悲しい

safe
anzen (na) — 安全（な）

safety pin
anzempin — 安全ピン

sake cup
sakazuki — 杯

ENGLISH-JAPANESE

salad
sarada
サラダ

salt
shio
塩

same
onaji
同じ

sandals
sandaru
サンダル

sandwich
sandoit·chi
サンドイッチ

sanitary towel
seiri·yō napkin
生理用
ナプキン

Saturday
doyōbi
土曜日

saucer
ukezara
受皿

sausage
sōsēji
ソーセージ

say
īmas
言います

school
gak·kō
学校

scissors
hasami
鋏

Scotland
Skot·torando
スコット
ランド

screwdriver
neji·mawashi
ねじまわし

scroll (*hanging*)
kakejik
掛け軸

sea
umi
海

seal: personal seal
hanko
はんこ

seaside: at the seaside
kaigan de
海岸で

seat
seki
席

seat belt
shīto beruto
シート
ベルト

seaweed
kaisō
海草

second (*in time*)
byō
秒

see
mimas
見ます

sell
urimas
売ります

sellotape (*R*)
serotēp
セロテープ

send
okurimas
送ります

separate
bets·bets (no)
別々（の）

September
kugats
九月

serviette
napkin
ナプキン

several
ikutska (no)
いくつか（の）

sew
nuimas
縫います

sexy
sekshī (na)
セクシー（な）

shade: in the shade
kage ni
陰に

shampoo
shampū
シャンプー

share (*cake etc*)
wakemas
分けます

ENGLISH-JAPANESE

to share a room
ai·beya ni
shimas
相部屋に
します

shaving brush
higesoriyō
burash
髭剃り用
ブラシ

shaving foam
shēbing·g
fōm
シェービン
グフォーム

she
kanojo; (see
grammar)
彼女

sheet
shīts
シーツ

Shinto
Shintō
神道

ship
fune
船

shirt
shats
シャツ

shoe laces
kuts·himo
靴紐

shoe polish
kutsuzumi
靴墨

shoe repairer
kutsu no
shūzen·ya
靴の修繕屋

shoes
kutsu
靴

shop
mise
店

**shopping: go
shopping**
kaimono ni
ikimas
買物に
行きます

short (*person*)
se no hikui
背の低い

(*time*)
mijikai
短い

shorts
pants
パンツ

shoulder
kata
肩

shower
shawā
シャワー

sick: I feel sick
haki·ke ga
shimas
吐き気が
します

sidewalk (*US*)
hodō
歩道

silk
kinu
絹

silver
gin
銀

silver foil
gimpak
銀箔

similar
onaji yō (na)
同じよう
（な）

since (*time*)
. . . kara
・・・から

single (*unmarried*)
dokshin (no)
独身（の）

sister (*older: own*)
ane
姉

(*someone else's*)
onē·san
お姉さん

(*younger: own*)
imōto
妹

(*someone else's*)
imōto·san
妹さん

sit down
suwarimas
座ります

size
saiz
サイズ

skin
hifu
皮膚

108

ENGLISH-JAPANESE

skinny
yasete — 痩せて

skirt
skāto — スカート

sky
sora — 空

sleep
nemurimas — 眠ります

sleeper
shindaisha — 寝台車

sleeping bag
nebukuro — 寝袋

sleeping pill
suimin·yak — 睡眠薬

sleepy: I'm sleepy
nemuku narimashta — 眠くなりました

slide (*phot*)
suraido — スライド

slim
hos·sori shte — ほっそりして

slippers
surip·pa — スリッパ

slow
noroi — のろい

slowly
yuk·kuri — ゆっくり

small
chīsai — 小さい

smell (*verb*)
nioimas — 匂います

smile (*verb*)
hoho·emimas — 頬笑みます

smoke
kemuri — 煙

smoke (*verb*)
tabako o suimas — タバコを吸います

snake
hebi — 蛇

snow
yuki — 雪

so: so pretty
totemo kirei — とてもきれい

not so much
son·na ni irimasen — そんなにいりません

soap
sek·ken — 石けん

socket
soket·to — ソケット

socks
sok·ks — ソックス

soft
yawarakai — 柔らかい

soft drink
softo dorink — ソフトドリンク

sole (*of shoe*)
kuts no soko — 靴の底

some
ikutsuka (no) — いくつか(の)

some wine/flour/biscuits
wain/komugiko/bisket·to o skoshi — ワイン／小麦粉／ビスケットを少し

somebody
dare ka — 誰か

something
nani ka — 何か

sometimes
tokidoki — 時々

ENGLISH-JAPANESE

son
musko·san 息子さん
(*own*)
musko 息子

song
uta 歌

soon
sugu すぐ

**sore: I've got a
sore throat**
nodo ga itai des 喉が痛い
です

soup
sūp スープ

sour
sup·pai 酸っぱい

south
minami 南

spanner
spana スパナ

spare parts
spea·pāto スペアパート

spark plug
spāk purag スパーク
プラグ

speak
hanashimas 話します
**do you speak
...?**
... ga ···がわ
wakarimas ka? かりますか？

speed limit
spīdo seigen スピード制限

spider
kumo 蜘蛛

spoon
spūn スプーン

spring (*season*)
haru 春

square (*in town*)
hiroba 広場

stairs
kaidan 階段

stamp
kit·te 切手

star
hoshi 星

station
eki 駅

stay (*in hotel etc*)
tomarimas 泊まります

steak
stēki ステーキ

steal
nusumimas 盗みます

steep
kyū (na) 急（な）

steering wheel
unten handoru 運転ハンドル

still (*sit etc*)
jit·to じっと
it's still raining
mada fut·te imas まだ降って
います

stockings
stok·king·g ストッキング

stomach
onaka お腹

stomach ache
fukutsū 腹痛

stone
ishi 石

stop
teiryūsho 停留所

stop (*verb*)
tomarimas 止まります

store (*shop*)
mise 店

110

ENGLISH-JAPANESE

storm
arashi — 嵐

story
hanashi — 話

straight ahead
mas·sugu it·te — 真っすぐ行って

strange
hen (na) — 変（な）

strawberry
ichigo — 苺

stream
nagare — 流れ

street
tōri — 通り

string
himo — 紐

stroke (*attack*)
nōsot·chū — 脳卒中

strong
tsyoi — 強い

student
gaksei — 学生

stupid
baka (na) — 馬鹿（な）

suburbs
kōgai — 郊外

subway
chikatets — 地下鉄

suddenly
totsuzen ni — 突然に

sugar
satō — 砂糖

suit
sūts — スーツ

suitcase
sūts·kēs — スーツケース

summer
nats — 夏

sun
taiyō — 太陽

sunburn
hiyake — 日焼け

Sunday
nichiyōbi — 日曜日

sunglasses
san·guras — サングラス

sunset
nichibots — 日没

sunstroke
nis·shabyō — 日射病

suntan lotion
santan rōshon — サンタンローション

supermarket
sūpā — スーパー

surname
myōji — 名字

sweater
sētā — セーター

sweet
okashi — お菓子

sweet (*to taste*)
amai — 甘い

swim
oyogimas — 泳ぎます

swimming costume
mizugi — 水着

swimming pool
pūru — プール

swimming trunks
suiei·pants — 水泳パンツ

switch
suit·chi — スイッチ

T

table tēburu	テーブル	**telegram** dempō	電報
table tennis tak·kyū	卓球	**telephone** denwa	電話
take torimas	取ります	**television** terebi	テレビ
take away (*remove*) tori·nozokimas	取り除きます	**temple** otera	お寺
talk hanashimas	話します	**tennis** tenis	テニス
tall (*person*) se no takai	背の高い	**tent** tento	テント
tap (*for water*) jaguchi	蛇口	**terrible** hidoi	ひどい
tape (*cassette*) tēp	テープ	**terrific** totemo ī	とてもいい
taxi takshī	タクシー	**than: uglier than** . . . . . . yorimo minikui	. . .より もみにくい
tea (*black*) kōcha (*green*) ocha	紅茶 お茶	**thank** kansha shimas	感謝します
teach oshiemas	教えます	**thank you** arigatō	ありがとう
teacher sensei	先生	**that** (*adjective*) ano (*pronoun*) are	あの あれ
teahouse chamise	茶店	**that one** are	あれ
team chīm	チーム	**the** (*see grammar*)	
teapot (*Japanese-style*) kyūs	急須	**theatre** gekijō	劇場
teapot (*Western-style*) tī pot·to	ティーポット	**their(s)** karera no; (*see grammar*)	彼らの
		them (*object: people*) karera o	彼らを

ENGLISH-JAPANESE

(things)
sorera o; *(see grammar)* それらを

then *(after)*
sorekara それから

there
soko de そこで

it's there
mukō ni arimas むこうに あります

there is/are . . . *(people)*
. . . ga imas ・・・が います

is/are there . . .? *(people)*
. . . ga imas ka? ・・・が いますか？

there isn't/aren't . . . *(people)*
. . . wa imasen ・・・は いません

there is/are . . . *(things)*
. . . ga arimas ・・・が あります

is/are there . . .? *(things)*
. . . ga arimas ka? ・・・があ りますか？

there isn't/aren't . . . *(things)*
. . . wa arimasen ・・・は ありません

thermometer *(for weather)*
kandankei 寒暖計

thermos flask
mahōbin 魔法ビン

these *(adjective)*
kono この

(pronoun)
kore これ

they
karera; *(see grammar)* 彼ら

thick
atsui 厚い

thief
dorobō 泥棒

thigh
momo 腿

thin *(person)*
yasete 痩せて

(thing)
usui 薄い

thing
mono 物

think
kangaemas 考えます

thirsty: I'm thirsty
nodo ga kawakimashta 喉が渇き ました

this *(adjective)*
kono この

(pronoun)
kore これ

this one
kore これ

those *(adjective)*
ano あの

(pronoun)
are あれ

thread
ito 糸

throat
nodo 喉

through
. . . o tōt·te ・・・を 通って

throw
nagemas 投げます

113

throw away sutemas	捨てます	**tobacco** tabako	タバコ
thunderstorm raiu	雷雨	**today** kyō	今日
Thursday mokuyōbi	木曜日	**toe** tsmasaki	爪先
ticket kip·pu	切符	**together** is·shoni	一緒に
tie nektai	ネクタイ	**toilet** toire	トイレ
tight kitsui	きつい	**toilet paper** toiret·to pēpā	トイレット ペーパー
tights taits	タイツ		
time jikan	時間	**tomato** tomato	トマト
on time jikan dōri	時間通り	**tomorrow** ashta	明日
what time is it? ima nanji des ka?	今何時 ですか？	**tongue** shta	舌
		tonight komban	今晩
timetable (transport) jikok·hyō	時刻表	**tonsillitis** hentōsen·en	扁桃腺炎
tin opener kankiri	缶切り	**too** (also) mo (excessively) ....sugimas	も ・・・過ぎます
tip chip·pu	チップ	**too big** ōki·sugimas	大き過ぎます
tire (US) taiya	タイヤ	**not too much** taksan de naku	たくさんでなく
tired tskarete	疲れて	**tooth** ha	歯
tissues tis·shū	ティシュー	**toothache** ha·ita	歯痛
to: I'm going to Nagoya/the station watashi wa Nagoya/eki e ikimas	私は名古屋 /駅へ行 きます	**toothbrush** haburash	歯ブラシ
		toothpaste hamigaki	歯磨き

ENGLISH-JAPANESE

torch
kaichū dentō 懐中電灯

tourist
ryokōsha 旅行者

towel
taoru タオル

town
machi 町

traditional
dentōteki (na) 伝統的（な）

traffic
kōtsū 交通

traffic jam
kōtsū jūtai 交通渋滞

traffic lights
shin·gō 信号

train
densha 電車

trainers
torēning·g トレーニン
shūz グシューズ

translate
hon·yak shimas 翻訳します

travel agent's
ryokō dairiten 旅行代理店

**traveller's
cheque**
toraberāz トラベラー
chek·k ズチェック

tree
ki 木

trip
tabi 旅

trousers
zubon ズボン

true
hontō (no) 本当（の）

trunk (*US: car*)
torank トランク

try
tameshimas 試します

T-shirt
tī shats ティー
シャツ

Tuesday
kayōbi 火曜日

tunnel
ton·neru トンネル

tweezers
kenuki 毛抜き

tyre
taiya タイヤ

U

ugly
minikui みにくい

umbrella
kasa 傘

uncle
oji·san おじさん
(*own*)
oji おじ

under (*spatially*)
... shta 下

underpants
pants パンツ

understand
wakarimas わかります

United States
Gas·shūkok 合衆国

university
daigaku 大学

unpleasant
fuyukai (na) 不愉快（な）

ENGLISH-JAPANESE

until
... made
・・・まで

up: up there
asoko ni
あそこに

upstairs
ue
上

urgent
kinkyū (no)
緊急（の）

us
watashtachi;
(see grammar)
私達

use
tskaimas
使います

useful
yūeki (na)
有益（な）

usually
futsū
普通

V

valid
yūkō (na)
有効（な）

valley
tani
谷

van
ban
バン

vanilla
banira
バニラ

vase
kabin
花瓶

VD
seibyō
性病

veal
ko·ushi no niku
小牛の肉

vegetarian
saishok
shugisha
菜食主義者

very
totemo
とても

very much
totemo
とても

video
bideo
ビデオ

village
mura
村

vinegar
su
酢

visa
biza
ビザ

visit (verb)
tazunemas
訪ねます

voice
koe
声

volcano
kazan
火山

W

waist
uesto
ウェスト

wait
machimas
待ちます

waiter
uētā
ウェーター

waitress
uētores
ウェートレス

wake up (oneself)
me o
samashimas
目を覚まします

Wales
Uēruz
ウェールズ

walk (verb)
arukimas
歩きます

walkman (R)
uōkman
ウォークマン

ENGLISH-JAPANESE

wall kabe	壁	**can you tell me the way to the …?** … e wa dō it·tara ī des ka?	・・・へは どう行った らいいです か？
wallet saifu	財布		
want hoshī	ほしい	**we** watashtachi; (see grammar)	私達
I want … watashi wa … ga hoshī des	私は・・・ がほしいです	**weak** yowai	弱い
do you want …? … ga hoshī des ka?	・・・がほし いですか？	**weather** tenki	天気
		wedding kek·kon shki	結婚式
war sensō	戦争	**Wednesday** suiyōbi	水曜日
warm atatakai	暖かい	**week** shū	週
it's warm atatakai des	暖かいです	**weekend** shūmats	週末
wash araimas	洗います	**weight** omosa	重さ
washbasin sem·men dai	洗面台	**welcome!** yōkoso	ようこそ
washing powder senzai	洗剤	**welcome: you're welcome** dō itashimashte	どういたし まして
washing·up liquid shok·ki yō senzai	食器用洗剤		
wasp hachi	蜂	**well: he's well** kare wa genki des	彼は元気 です
watch (for time) tokei	時計		
watch (verb) mimas	見ます	**well: he's not well** kare wa genki dewa arimasen	彼は元気 ではあり ません
water mizu	水		
way: this way (like this) kō shte	こうして	**well** (adverb) jōzuni	上手に

117

ENGLISH-JAPANESE

west
nishi — 西

Western-style
yōfū — 洋風

wet
nurete — 濡れて

what?
nani? — 何 ?

what...? (*which*)
dono...? — どの・・・?

what's this?
kore wa nan des ka? — これは何ですか ?

wheel
sharin — 車輪

when?
its? — いつ?

where?
doko? — どこ?

which?
dochira? — どちら ?

white
shiroi — 白い

who?
dare? — だれ ?

whose: whose is this?
kore wa dare no des ka? — これはだれのですか ?

why?
dōshte? — どうして?

wide
hiroi — 広い

wife
ok·san — 奥さん

(*own*)
kanai — 家内

win
kachimas — 勝ちます

wind
kaze — 風

window
mado — 窓

windscreen
furonto garas — フロントガラス

wine
wain — ワイン

winter
fuyu — 冬

wire
waiya — ワイヤ

with
... to is·sho ni — ・・・と一緒に

without
... nashi de — ・・・なしで

woman
josei — 女性

wonderful
subarashī — すばらしい

wood (*material*)
zaimok — 材木

wool
yōmō — 羊毛

word
kotoba — 言葉

work (*verb*)
hatarakimas — 働きます

it's not working
sadō shte imasen — 作動していません

ENGLISH-JAPANESE

world
sekai — 世界

worse
mot·to warui — もっと悪い

wrench
renchi — レンチ

wrist
tekubi — 手首

write
kakimas — 書きます

wrong
machigat·te — 間違って

Y

year
toshi — 年

yellow
kīroi — 黄色い

yes
hai — はい

oh yes I do!
mochiron des — もちろんです

yesterday
kinō — 昨日

yet: not yet
mada des — まだです

yoghurt
yōguruto — ヨーグルト

you
anata — あなた
(*plural*)
anatatachi — あなたたち
(*object*)
anata o; (*see grammar*) — あなたを

young
wakai — 若い

young people
wakamono — 若者

your(s)
anata no — あなたの
(*plural*)
anatatachi no; — あなたた
(*see grammar*) — ちの

Z

Zen Buddhism
Zen — 禅

zero
zero — ゼロ

zip
fasnā — ファスナー

zoo
dōbutsu·en — 動物園

GRAMMAR

ARTICLES

'A' and 'the' are not translated in Japanese:

ginkō
a bank, the bank

PLURALS

Singulars and plurals are not differentiated:

Nihon-jin
a Japanese person, the Japanese people

ADJECTIVES

ōkī	big
ōkī des	it is big
ōkī machi des	it is a big town

These adjectives, ending in **i**, take past and negative forms:

atsui des	it is hot
atsku nai des	it is not hot
atskat-ta des	it was hot
atsku nakat-ta des	it was not hot

Other adjectives, not ending in **i**, do not change:

shizka des	it's quiet
shizka deshta	it was quiet

but, when preceding a noun, are linked to it by **na** or **no**:

shizka na tokoro des   it is a quiet place

There are no *COMPARATIVE* or *SUPERLATIVE* forms for adjectives:

who is taller? = who is tall?
dochira ga takai des ka?

'Than' is translated by **yori**:

Tōkyō wa Ōsaka yori ōkī des
Tokyo is bigger than Osaka

120

GRAMMAR

'More', when it is necessary, is translated by **mot-to**:

> **mot-to yuk-kri hanashte kudasai**
> please speak more slowly

'Most' is translated by **mot-tomo** or **ichiban** (= number one):

> **mot-tomo hayai des**   it's the quickest

PERSONAL PRONOUNS are often not required. They are understood from the context:

> **ikimas ka? – hai, ikimas**   are you going? – yes, I am

The forms are:

watashi	I	**watashtachi**	we
anata	you	**anatatachi**	you (*plural*)
kare, kanojo	he, she	**karera**	they (*masculine*)
		kanojora	they (*feminine*)
		sorera	they (*things*)

The pronoun 'it' in sentences like 'did you see it?' is normally not translated.

These forms are also used for 'me, him' etc as in:

> **watashi des**   it's me

If a pronoun *is* used as a subject it is followed by the particle **wa** or **ga**. As a direct object it is followed by **o**. And as an indirect object it is followed by **ni**:

> **watashi o shit·te imas**   **kare ni age·mashta**
> he knows me   I gave it to him

POSSESSIVE ADJECTIVES and *POSSESSIVE PRONOUNS* are the same in Japanese. **No** is added to the pronoun to express possession:

watashi no	my/mine	**watashtachi**	our(s)
anata no	your(s)	**anatatachi**	your(s) (plural)
kare no	his	**karera no**	their(s) (*masculine*)
kanojo no	her(s)	**kanojora no**	their(s) (*feminine*)
		sorera no	their(s) (*of things*)

anata no tomodachi	**watashi no des**
your friend	it is mine

GRAMMAR

VERBS are almost completely regular. However, there are many inflexions, both for present and past tenses and for informal and respectful speech. But within each tense there are no distinctions for person. So for example:

ikimas

can mean, depending on context, all of:

I/you/we/they go, he/she/it goes

Japanese are sensitive to formality and courtesy in speech, and it is particularly in the verb forms that these are apparent. Perhaps a sensitivity to dress is equivalent in Britain, with its gradations from tails to jeans.

iras-shaimas ka?
ikimas ka?   are you going?
iku ka?

The longer the form, the politer it tends to be. It is best perhaps at first to speak at the intermediate levels. Verbs in this book are in this form.

EXPRESSING THE PRESENT

To express a continuing state, a compound form is used, as in English. To form this, replace the **-mas** from the form as given in the dictionary with **-te** and add the word **imas**:

mimas - to look   **shimas** - to do
terebi o mite imas   **kek-kon shte imas**
he is watching television   he is married
                                   (literally: he does marriage)

Some common verbs are irregular:

kakimas - to write — **kaite**
yomimas - to read — **yonde**
aimas - to meet — **at-te**
kirimas - to cut — **kit-te**

Other verbs with these endings follow the same pattern. Note also the following:

ikimas - to go — **it-te**

EXPRESSING THE FUTURE

The future is expressed, as it sometimes is in English, by a present form:

ashta kimas   he comes tomorrow

GRAMMAR

EXPRESSING THE PAST

The past tense can be formed from the verbs as given in the
dictionary as follows:

	present	past
positive	**ikimas**	**ikimashta**
negative	**ikimasen**	**ikimasen deshta**

> **kinō Amerika e kaerimashta**
> he returned yesterday to the States

PERMISSION

To ask permission to do something you can use the
construction . . . **ī des ka?**. In front of this you place the verb
with the following change: replace the **-mas** as given in the
dictionary with **-te**

> **mimas** - to look
>
> **mite ī des ka?**
> can I see?
> (literally: seeing is good?)

NECESSITY

To say that you have to do something, or that someone has to
do something, remove the **-imas** from the verb and add **-anakereba narimasen**:

> **ikimas** - to go
>
> **ikanakereba narimasen**
> I have to go
> (literally: if not go, won't do)

WANTING

To say that you want to do something, or that someone wants
to do something, replace the **-mas** of the verb with **-tai**:

> **ikimas** - to go
>
> **ikitai des**
> I want to go

The verb *TO BE* is **des**. The forms are:

	present	past
positive	**des**	**deshta**
negative	**dewa arimasen**	**dewa arimasen deshta**

> **sensei des**
> I'm/you're/he/she is a teacher
> we're/they're teachers

> **hoteru dewa arimasen deshta**
> it wasn't a hotel, it didn't use to be a hotel

GRAMMAR

THERE IS/ARE

'There is/are' is translated by **arimas** for lifeless objects, by **imas** for living things. The forms are:

	present	*past*
positive	**arimas**	**arimashta**
negative	**arimasen**	**arimasen deshta**

	present	*past*
positive	**imas**	**imashta**
negative	**imasen**	**imasen deshta**

> **kip-pu ga arimas ka?**
> are there any tickets?

> **oisha-san ga imas ka?**
> is there a doctor here?

Many Japanese verbs are derived from Chinese, especially verbs used in public rather than domestically, like English verbs derived from French. These verbs are linked to **shimas**, 'to do' or 'to make', and only the **shimas** changes:

> **ryokō shimas/ryokō shimashta**
> travel/travelled

YES/NO

'Yes' is **hai**, 'no' is **īe**. But **hai** may also be used where English uses 'no':

> **do you like chocolate?**
> hai, ski des — yes, I do

> **don't you like chocolate?**
> hai, ski dewa arimasen — no, I don't

The *NEGATIVES* 'never', 'nowhere', 'nobody' and 'nothing' are translated by:

> when?/where?/who?/what? + 'also' + negative verb:

> **its mo banana o tabemasen**
> I never eat bananas

> **dare mo shirimasen**
> I don't know anybody

GRAMMAR

To form a *QUESTION* ka is placed at the end of a sentence:

kore des	it's this one
kore des ka?	is it this one?

Here are some useful question words:

who — **dare; donata** (politer)
dare des ka   who is it?

what — **nan**
nan des ka?   what is it?

where — **doko**
doko des ka?   where is it?

how — **dō**
dō shimas ka?   how do I do it?

how much — **ikra**
ikra des ka?   how much is it?

why — **naze**
naze ikimasen ka?   why are you not going?

when — **its**
its kaerimas ka?   when do you come back?

COUNT WORDS

Japanese uses two sets of numbers, Chinese and the original Japanese numbers up to ten:

	Chinese	*Japanese*
1	**ichi**	**hitots**
2	**ni**	**ftats**
3	**san**	**mit-ts**
4	**shi**	**yot-ts**
5	**go**	**itsuts**
6	**rok**	**mut-ts**
7	**shichi**	**nanats**
8	**hachi**	**yat-ts**
9	**kyū**	**kokonots**
10	**jū**	**tō**

Either system can be used with nouns, but they are used in different ways. The Chinese numbers require an additional counter, like the English *'a bowl* of soup, *'a cup* of tea'; the Japanese numbers do not. The use of Japanese numbers is normally restricted to smallish, domestic items and for expressions of age.

GRAMMAR

Different types of object require different counters, for example:

> *counters for:*
> animals   **hiki**
> fruit, round objects   **ko**
> pieces of paper, tickets etc   **mai**
> people   **nin**

> **hambāgā o san*ko* kudasai**
> **hambāgā o mit-ts kudasai**
> three hamburgers please

> **kip-pu o ni*mai***
> two tickets

> **kyōdai ga yo*nin* imas**
> I have four brothers

Beyond ten, only the Chinese numbers are used:

> 11 children
> **kodomo jūichi-nin**

PARTICLES

There are several short particles. These come at the end of a word or phrase and indicate how it relates to the rest of the sentence:

wa or **ga** usually indicate the subject of a sentence. If the weight of the sentence falls on the subject, **ga** is used: otherwise, **wa**:

> **Tanaka-san ga kimashta**
> Mr Tanaka came (not somebody else)

> **Tanakasan wa ashita kimas**
> Mr Tanaka comes tomorrow

o indicates the object of a verb:

> **kore o kudasai**
> please give me this one

ni is used for 'to':

> **Nihon ni kaerimas**
> I return to Japan

GRAMMAR

or for 'in' when there is no idea of activity involved:

> **Tōkyō ni sunde imas**
> I live in Tokyo

de is used for 'in' (when there is an idea of activity):

> **kōba de hataraite imas**
> he works in a factory

it is also used for 'by means of':

> **bas de ikimas**
> I'll go by bus

e is used for 'to':

> **Ōsaka e hikōki de kaerimas**
> I go back to Osaka by plane

to is used for 'with', 'and':

> **hambāgā to kōhī kudasai**
> hamburger and a coffee please

no is used for 'of':

> **kruma no iro**
> the colour of the car
> (literally: car of colour)

> **hikōki no jikan**
> the time of the flight

mo is used for 'too':

> **watashi mo mimashta**
> I saw it too

> **Kyōto mo ikitai des**
> I (etc) would like to go to Kyoto too

CONVERSION TABLES

metres
  1 metre = 39.37 inches or 1.09 yards

kilometres
1 kilometre = 0.62 or approximately ⅝ mile

to convert kilometres to miles: divide by 8 and multiply by 5

kilometres:	2	3	4	5	10	100
miles:	1.25	1.9	2.5	3.1	6.25	62.5

miles
to convert miles to kilometres: divide by 5 and multiply by 8

miles:	1	3	5	10	20	100
kilometres:	1.6	4.8	8	16	32	160

kilos
  1 kilo = 2.2 or approximately 1⅕ pounds

to convert kilos to pounds: divide by 5 and multiply by 11

kilos:	4	5	10	20	30	40
pounds:	8.8	11	22	44	66	88

pounds
  1 pound = 0.45 or approximately 5⁄11 kilo

litres
  1 litre = approximately 1¾ pints or 0.22 gallons

Celsius
to convert to Fahrenheit: divide by 5, multiply by 9, add 32

Celsius:	10	15	20	25	28	30	34
Fahrenheit:	50	59	68	77	82	86	93

Fahrenheit
to convert Fahrenheit to Celsius: subtract 32, multiply by 5,
divide by 9